BASIC KEYBOARDING APPLICATIONS

Centering, Tables, & Forms

DR. LLOYD W. BARTHOLOME
PROFESSOR AND HEAD
DEPARTMENT OF BUSINESS EDUCATION
AND ADMINISTRATIVE SYSTEMS
UTAH STATE UNIVERSITY
LOGAN, UTAH

DR. MARION B. HOLMES
DIRECTOR OF VOCATIONAL EDUCATION
SCHOOL DISTRICT OF PHILADELPHIA

Copyright © 1984
by South-Western Publishing Co.
Cincinnati, Ohio

ISBN: 0-538-20371-4

Library of Congress Catalog Card Number: 83-60197

23456789HO9876

Printed in the United States of America

Published by

SOUTH-WESTERN PUBLISHING CO.

CINCINNATI   WEST CHICAGO, ILL.   DALLAS   PELHAM MANOR, N.Y.   PALO ALTO, CALIF.

Dear Student:

You will learn to center information attractively on a page as you work through this booklet. You also will learn to type several kinds of business forms. These skills will help you apply your typing to job situations and for personal use.

This booklet is designed as a complete learning system. There will be no daily assignments. You should be able to complete all parts by carefully reading and following instructions. You will work at your own pace, without waiting for other students. If you have questions, ask your teacher. To make your learning easier, this booklet has the following helps:

1. **GOALS:** Read the goals to learn what you will be able to do after studying and typing the jobs in each of the four units.

2. **ROAD SIGNS:** Follow the road signs in the left column. They are a quick guide which tell you what to do.

Make machine adjustments.

Read for explanations and directions.

Study or answer questions.

Type drills and jobs.

If you can check "Yes," continue. If you check "No," retype, make the necessary corrections, or ask for help.

Check "Yes" if you answered the questions correctly or you understand your mistake(s). Check "No" if you do not understand your mistakes; get help from teacher before continuing.

Turn in for teacher approval. Check "Yes" if you received approval. Check "No" if you have to retype or do makeup work. Applies to challenge jobs and tests.

3. **SMALL ILLUSTRATIONS:** Study and use these examples. They show how to arrange the problem or new learning on the page.

4. **CHALLENGE JOB:** Check your skill on each unit before taking a test on it. Give this job to your teacher for approval. If you are successful with the *Challenge Job*, you are ready to take the unit test.

5. **REVIEW—KEY CONCEPTS:** Complete the statements by filling in the blanks. The questions cover the main points from the unit.

6. **TESTS:** Take a test on the skills you learned in each unit to see how well you can set up and accurately type a job that is like those you have typed in the unit.

7. **APPENDIX:** This section reviews basic procedures that you follow when you type tables and forms. The *Appendix* contains the following items:

Word-Division Guides: Study these guides and complete the exercises on page 72.

Learning to Listen for the Bell: Your typewriter has a bell to warn you when the right margin is near. Complete Drills 1 and 2 before beginning Unit 1.

Correction Techniques: Check this section for directions on the use of erasers, correction paper, correction fluid, and lift-off tape/ribbon.

Proofreader's Marks: Study these marks and make sure that you understand each symbol before you type rough-draft copy. The chart with these symbols appears on page 75.

Answer Checkup: Answers to *Review: Key Concepts* and other short questions appear on pages 75-77.

Student Check Sheet: This chart will help you keep track of your progress by recording the date you complete each job and rating your work with a +, √, or −.

8. **TYPING RULER:** Use the ruler on the inside back cover to see if your work is well placed on the page. The first illustration shows the number of typewritten lines if copy is single-spaced (Lines 1-60). The other illustration measures the number of strokes in pica or elite type.

YOU ARE NOW READY TO BEGIN! HAVE FUN!

CENTERING, TABLES, AND FORMS

When you plan the placement of the title of a report, set the margins on your typewriter, or prepare a table or a business form, you must understand how to center horizontally (across) the page. Your goal is to put the same amount of white space on both the left and the right sides of the copy. You want the left and right margins to be equal or as close to equal as possible.

In CENTERING, TABLES, AND FORMS, you will learn how to center copy horizontally. Once you know how to do this, you will learn how to center copy vertically (up and down) so that you will be able to type work that has equal white space on the top and bottom, as well as in the left and right margins. You will apply your centering skills to preparing tables and arranging information attractively on different kinds of business forms.

WOMEN IN THE WORKFORCE

For the first time, women in 1980 working outside the home outnumbered housewives. By 1990, it is projected that working women will make up about 60 percent of the workforce.[1]

Why Do Women Work?

The main reason women work is for money and necessity. Three out of five working women are single, separated, widowed, divorced, or married to unemployed men.

Where Are Women Employed?

Women are employed as clerical workers, service workers, and as professional and technical workers. Only a small percentage of women are employed as managers.

Yet, women who are interested in upward mobility within a firm may advance. Today over half of the businesses have programs for hiring, training, and promoting women executives. Managerial positions, however, often require strong commitment as noted below:

> Women are also finding that the achievement of "success" demands a commitment to long hours, a tolerance of mental stress and fatigue, and absence from family. And, some of the most exciting jobs in industry require frequent relocation or extensive travel.[2]

[1]John W. Wright, The American Almanac of Jobs and Salaries (New York: Avon Books, 1982), p. 710.

[2]Jeanine Rhea, "Opportunities for Women in Business: Better than Ever," Business Education Forum 35 (April 1981):26.

UNITED STATES' LARGEST BUILDINGS

Building	Stories
Sears Tower	110
World Trade Center	110
Empire State	102
Standard Oil	80
John Hancock Center	100

Krantz and Ross, Inc.
696 Tusculum Highway
Arcadia, WV 25967-3558
304-641-9327

PURCHASE ORDER

Purchase order No. 7273

Kiley's Printers, Inc.
69 Reservation Drive
Sinclair, NM 88435-3104

Date November 10, 19--
Terms 30 days net
Ship Via Shipping

Quantity	Cat. No.	Description	Price	Total
24 dozen	164-PB	Promotional ball point pens	$ 4.20	$100.80
5 reams	131-S5	Custom imprinted stationery	15.95	79.75
2 boxes	131-S5a	Matching custom envelopes	13.95	27.90
				$208.45
				+ 3.50
				$211.95

HORIZONTAL CENTERING

When you complete Unit 1, you will be able to center copy horizontally on any size of paper.

PART 1 GOAL

To be able to center copy horizontally on regular-size paper.

JOB 1   LEARNING TO CENTER HORIZONTALLY

2 Half sheets

READ → Horizontally means *across*. To help you remember this, think of the sun setting on the horizon— setting across the sky. Whenever you center horizontally, follow the steps below.

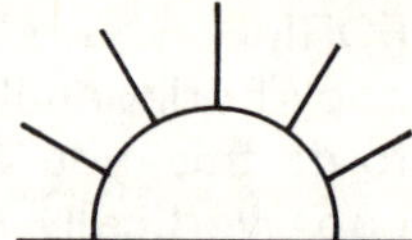

> **HORIZONTAL CENTERING GUIDE**
>
> 1. Tab to the center of the paper.
>
> 2. From the center, backspace 1 space for every 2 characters—letters, spaces, figures, or punctuation marks. Do not backspace for a "leftover" letter or figure at the end of the line.
>
> 3. Begin to type where the backspacing ends.

GET READY

1. Prepare your machine for centering:

   a. Set the paper guide so the left edge of the paper is at 0. Insert your half sheet of paper long side up with the left edge at 0.

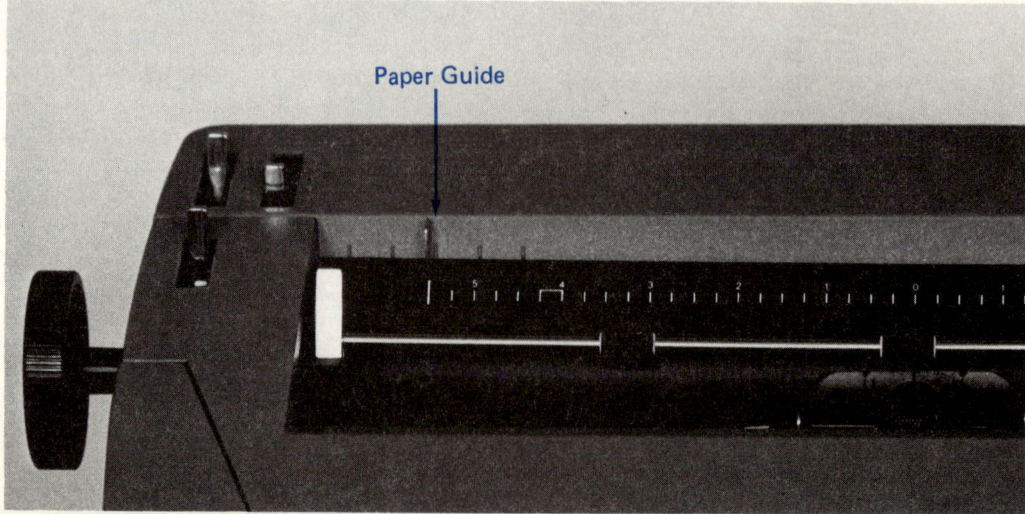

b. Find the center of a line by adding the figure at the left edge of the paper (0) to the figure at the right edge. Then, divide the sum by 2. Drop any fraction remaining.

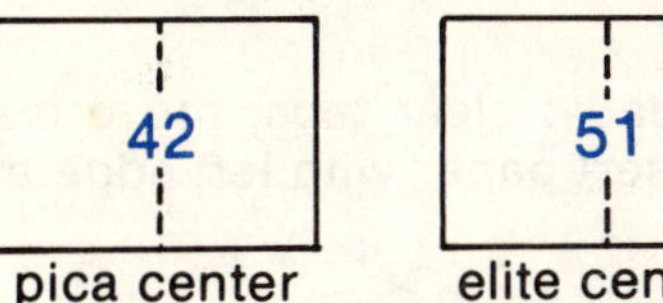

Pica center: 0 + 85 = 85 ÷ 2 = 42½ or 42
10 pica characters = 1 inch

Elite center: 0 + 102 = 102 ÷ 2 = 51
12 elite characters = 1 inch

c. Clear all tab stops. Move the left margin stop to 0 and the right margin stop to the end of the scale. Set a tab stop at the center of the paper.

2. Space down from the top edge of the paper 14 times. Following the *Horizontal Centering Guide* (page 2), center Line 1 of Drill 1 (below).

NOTE: In the illustration below, the symbol # stands for the space between words.

	KN	OW	#T	HE	SE	#T	YP	EW	RI	TE	R#	PA	RT	S
Backspace from center	1	2	3	4	5	6	7	8	9	10	11	12	13	—

3. Are you at the proper space: Pica, 29; elite, 38? Now, type Line 1 from this space.

4. Triple-space (TS), leaving 2 blank lines, after Line 1. Center and type Line 2 in the same way. Double-space (DS), leaving 1 blank line, as you type each of the other lines.

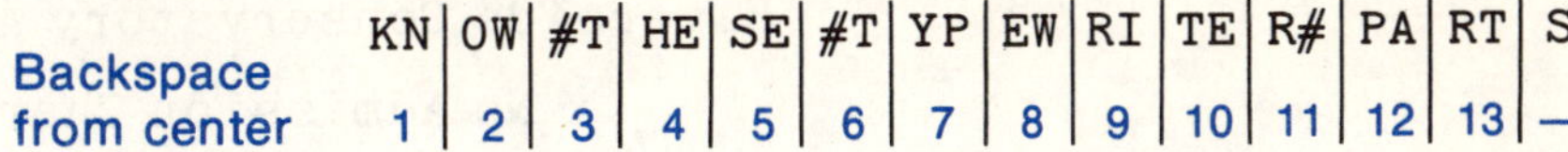

5. Take your paper out of your machine. There is a typing ruler inside the back cover of this book. Use it now to see if there is equal or almost equal space on each side of each line.

Drill 1

KNOW THESE TYPEWRITER PARTS
TS

Paper Bail
DS
Right Cylinder Knob

Drill 2

DICTATION EQUIPMENT
TS

Portable
DS
Desk Top
DS
Centralized Systems

6. Type Drill 2 in the same way. Insert your second half sheet in your typewriter. Begin on Line 13.

7. After you typed Drill 2, check to see that you have centered the drill correctly. Use the *Student Check Sheet*, p. 79, to rate your typing.

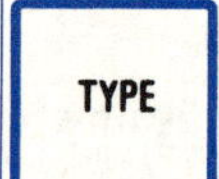

JOB 2   PRACTICE HORIZONTAL CENTERING

Half sheet

1. Get your machine ready: clear tabs; move margin stops to the left and right ends of the scale; insert paper with left edge at 0; set a tab at the center of the paper.

2. Starting on Line 11, horizontally center and type each line of Job 2. Follow the spacing directions.

A FINE ARTS RECITAL
TS

by
DS
The Desmond Quartet

Sunday, May 22, at 4:00 p.m.

Riverside Conservatory Auditorium

No Admission Charge

3. After you have typed the job, proofread and circle your errors. Use the ruler in the back to check your horizontal centering. Is there equal or almost equal space to the left and right of each line?

JOB 3   CENTERING FROM SCRIPT *(turn in for teacher approval)*

Half sheet

NOTE: *Correct all errors.* In Job 3 and all other *turn-in* or *challenge* jobs in this book, correct all errors. Before you remove your paper from your machine, proofread to be sure that all errors are corrected. See *Correction Techniques* in the Appendix.

1. Beginning on Line 9, center and type each line of Job 3. Follow the spacing directions given.

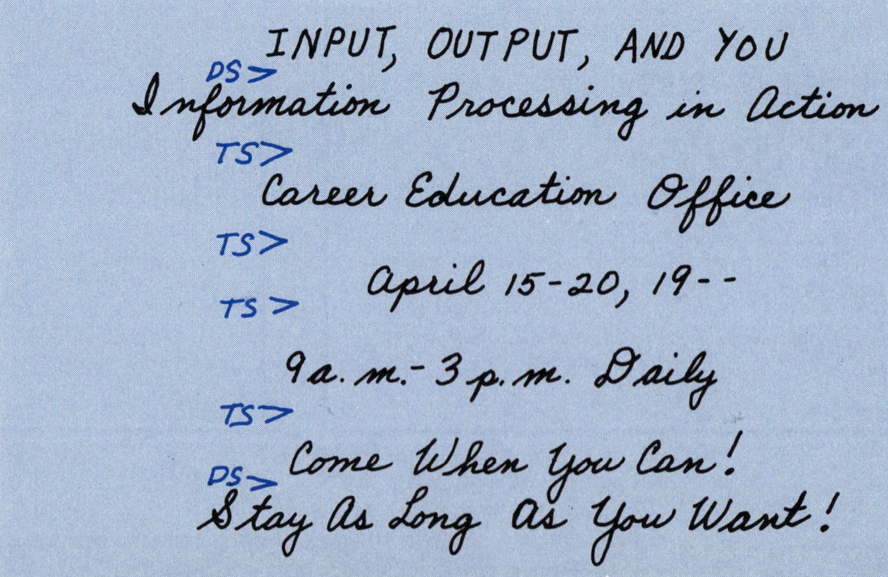

2. Check your finished copy. Is there equal or almost equal space before and after each typed line? Turn in Job 3 to your teacher for approval.

To be able to center horizontally on paper of different widths.

JOB 4   CENTERING ON OFF-SIZE PAPER

Half sheet (short side up)

1. Prepare your machine for centering: insert the half sheet with the short side at the top (shown below); set a tab stop at the center of the paper.

___________	Left edge of paper
+ ________	Plus right edge of paper
___________	Total
÷ 2	Divide total by 2
___________	Center

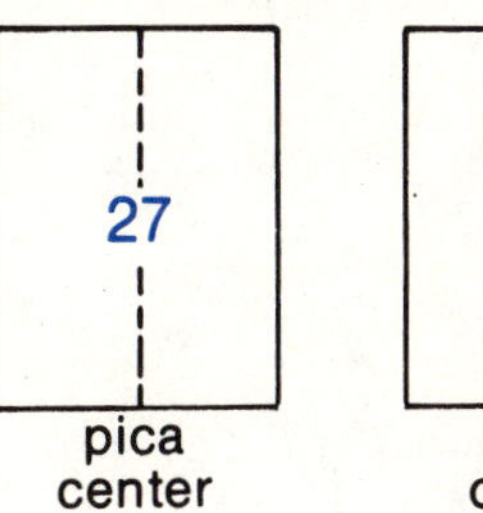
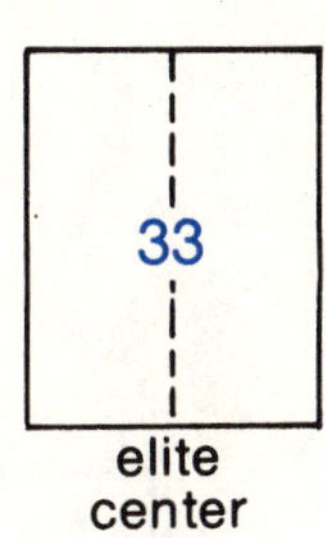

2. Check on page 75 of your *Answer Checkup* to see if your center is correct.

3. Beginning on Line 20, center each line of the job below. Follow the spacing directions given.

EFFECTIVE SUPERVISION IN TODAY'S OFFICE
TS >
9:30 a.m. - 4:15 p.m.
DS >
September 5, 19--
DS >
Information Processing Association
DS >
The Kimberly House
DS >
Madison, Wisconsin

YES____ **PROOFREAD/CHECK** ____NO

Continue   Ask for help

4. Proofread and circle errors. Then, use your ruler to check your centering on all lines. Is there equal or almost equal space on each side of each line?

JOB 5   CENTERING ON VARIOUS-LENGTH LINES

Form 1, page 123

1. A form is provided on page 123 in the back to type Job 5. When you insert the form in your typewriter, be sure that the form is in straight.

2. Prepare your machine for centering: Clear tabs and margins.

3. As you see on the form, the lines for typing this job are of different lengths. Each line will have a different center. To find the center of each one, follow the steps below. Use the spaces provided to find your centers.

   a. Read the scale at the left edge of the line.

   b. Read the scale at the right edge of the line and add this figure to the figure you found in Step *a*.

   c. Divide the total by 2. Your answer is the center point of the line.

	Line 1	Line 2	Line 3	Line 4	Line 5
Left edge of line	___	___	___	___	___
Plus right edge	+ ___	+ ___	+ ___	+ ___	+ ___
Total	___	___	___	___	___
Divide by 2	÷ 2	÷ 2	÷ 2	÷ 2	÷ 2
Center	___	___	___	___	___

TYPE

4. Follow the instructions on the form to type Job 5.

JOB 6 CHALLENGE JOB *(turn in for teacher approval)*

Half sheet (short side up)

Job 6 is a CHALLENGE job. It is a review before you take your first test on horizontal centering. Remember to correct errors on this and all challenge jobs.

TYPE

1. Prepare your machine for centering: clear tab stops; insert your paper; set a tab stop at the center of your paper. Beginning on Line 19, center and type each line of the job below. Try to finish Job 6 in 10 minutes or less.

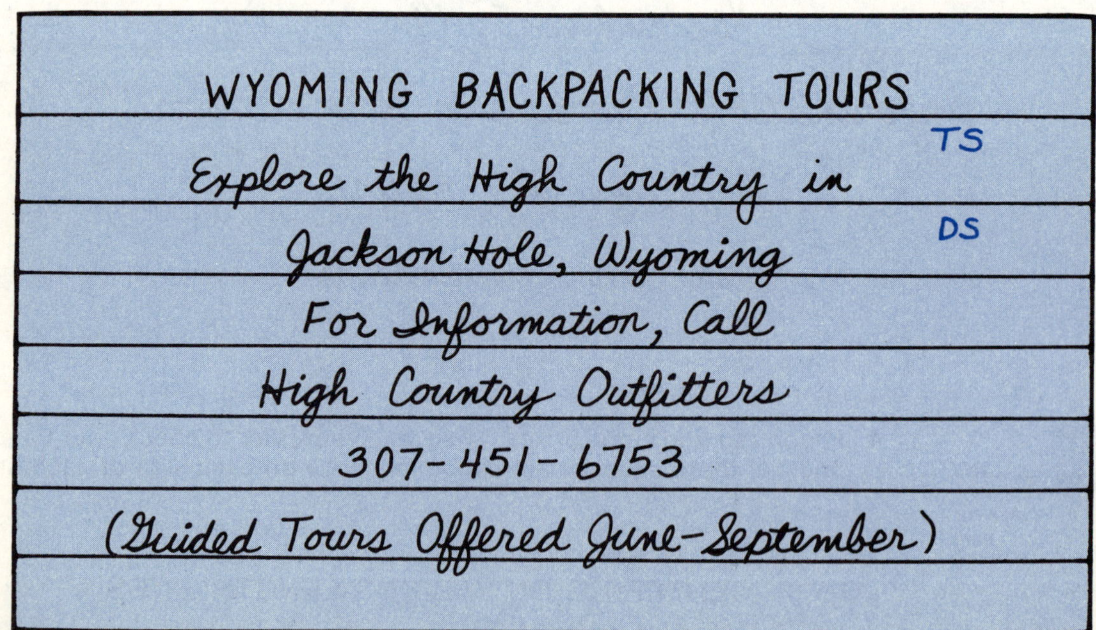

YES___ PROOFREAD/CHECK **___NO**

Continue   Ask for help

2. Leave your paper in your typewriter. Proofread your work and correct any errors you may have overlooked. Check with your ruler to see if your margins are equal or nearly equal. Then, turn in Job 6 to your teacher.

Fill in the blanks.

1. Horizontal means ___________________________.

2. Before you center, set the paper guide so the left edge of the paper is at ___________.

3. To find the center of a sheet of paper, _____________________ the figure at the left edge of the paper to the figure at the right edge. Divide the total by ___________.

4. On a pica typewriter, there are _____________________ spaces in a horizontal inch.

5. On an elite typewriter, there are _____________________ spaces in a horizontal inch.

6. Which typewriter are you using, pica or elite? _____________________.

7. To center a line horizontally, begin backspacing from the _____________________ of the paper.

8. When centering several lines horizontally, the typist should set a tab stop at the _____________________ of the paper.

9. When you center a line horizontally, backspace ___________ space(s) for each two letters, spaces, or punctuation marks in the line.

10. The horizontal center of a full sheet of paper is ___________ pica spaces.

11. The horizontal center of a full sheet of paper is ___________ elite spaces.

12. A triple space allows for ___________ blank lines between lines of type.

13. A double space allows for ___________ blank line(s) between lines of type.

14. The horizontal center of a sheet of paper 5½" wide is ___________ pica spaces.

15. The horizontal center of a 3-inch line is ___________ elite spaces.

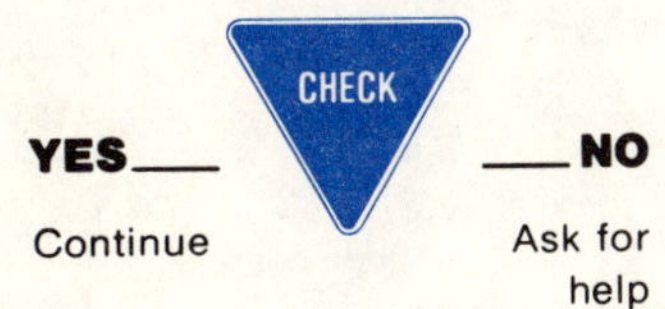

Now, check your answers in the Answer Checkup on page 75. Correct any answers you may have missed. If you do not understand an answer, ask your teacher for help.

Half sheet (long side up)

1. Center and type the following job on a half sheet of paper. Begin on Line 9 and follow the spacing directions given. Correct all errors neatly. Try to complete the job in 10 minutes or less.

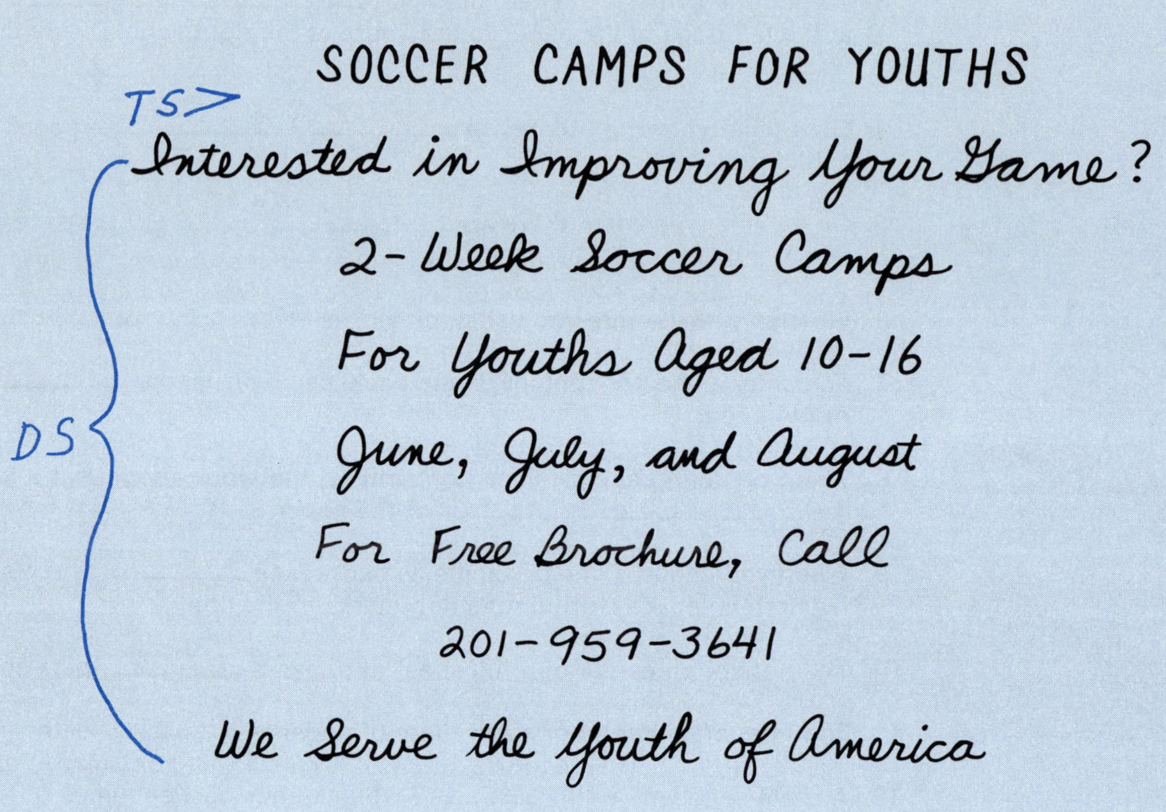

2. Leave your paper in your machine. Proofread one more time. If you missed any errors, correct them now. Did you finish within 10 minutes?

3. Turn in your test to your teacher.

VERTICAL CENTERING

When you complete Unit 2, you will be able to type copy with equal top and bottom margins. This skill is called *vertical* (up and down) centering.

PART 1 GOAL

To center typed copy vertically and horizontally on a half sheet.

When you center copy vertically on the page, insert the paper into the typewriter evenly so that the copy will look attractive on the page. Be sure the top of your paper is even with the top of the centering scale on the typewriter. See the illustration below to find the centering scale on your typewriter.

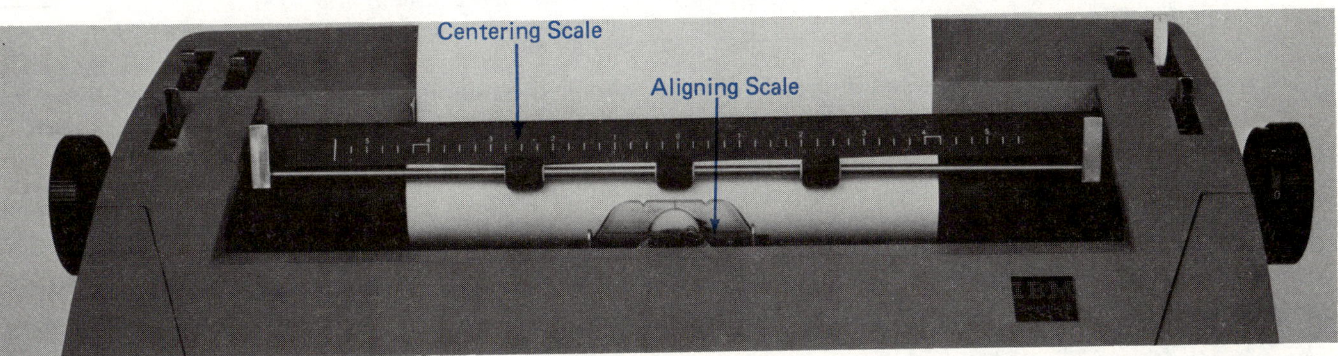

Read the guide below to learn the proper way to center copy vertically on the page. This guide applies to any size paper.

GUIDE FOR VERTICAL CENTERING

1. Find the total number of vertical lines available on the paper. There are 6 lines to 1 vertical inch; 33 lines to a half sheet, long side up; or 66 lines to a full sheet.

2. Count the number of lines in the job. Include both lines to be typed *and* blank lines between.

3. Subtract the number of lines needed to type the job from the lines on the paper. The difference represents the blank lines that will be divided between the top and bottom margins.

4. Divide the unused lines by 2 to get the top and bottom margins. Drop any fractions.

5. Space down from the top edge *one more line* than the number of lines to be left in the top and bottom margins. This will bring you to the line on which you will begin to type.

Example:

Lines on half sheet	33
Lines in job	−12
Unused lines	21
21 ÷ 2 = 10½ or 10	10
	+ 1
Begin to type on Line	11

JOB 1 LEARNING TO CENTER VERTICALLY

Half sheet (long side up)

1. Insert paper so that the top edge is even with the aligning scale (see page 9). Begin to count the lines for your top margin from this point.

2. Plan and set your margins for a 50-space line. If you need help to set your margins, go to page 73 in the *Appendix*. Show your figures below for finding both margins.

———— Center of paper		———— Center of paper	
− ———— Minus ½ the spaces in line		+ ———— Plus ½ the spaces in line	
———— Left margin		———— Right margin	

3. Set a tab to indent 5 spaces for typing a new paragraph. Set the line-space selector on SS.

4. Determine the vertical center for Job 1, following the steps below.

   a. Find the lines available on a half sheet (5½″ × 6 lines/inch) ————

   b. Count lines needed to type Job 1
   (Remember: DS = 1 blank line; TS = 2 blank lines) ————

   c. Subtract lines needed to type problem from lines available on the paper ————

   d. Divide by 2 (disregard the remaining one half) ————

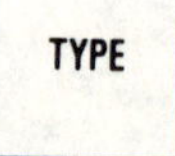

   e. Add 1 line. Begin to type on Line ————

5. Beginning on Line 11, center the heading. Then, type the rest of the job. When you finish typing, proofread and circle any errors you may have made.

```
 1
 2
 3
 4
 5
 6
 7
 8
 9
10
11              WHAT IS VERTICAL CENTERING?            1
12                                                     2
13                             TS                      3
14        Typed material which is centered vertically  4
15    has equal or almost equal top and bottom margins.5
16    Use vertical centering when typed copy should appear 6
17    especially neat and attractive on a page.        7
18                             DS                       8
19        The typist must decide when to center typed   9
20    copy vertically.  When and how to center vertically 10
21    will be an easy decision for those who have had good 11
22    typewriting instruction.                         12
23
24
25
26
27
28
29
30
31
32
33
```

JOB 2 CENTERING VERTICALLY AND HORIZONTALLY

Half sheet (long side up)

READ

Job 2 has both a main and a secondary heading. Type the main heading, *TABLE OF EXCUSES*, in ALL CAPS. For the subheading, *Anonymous*, capitalize the first letter only. DS between the main heading and the subheading. TS after the complete heading.

1. Prepare machine for centering: Clear tabs and margins; set line-space selector at SS; insert paper evenly, using the centering scale as a guide.

DO

2. On a half sheet of paper, center Job 2 vertically. The spacing directions are given on the job. Use the spaces below to figure your vertical centering.

   a. Lines available on a half sheet (5½″ × 6 lines/inch)   ———

   b. Lines needed to type Job 2   ———

   c. Lines which will be blank (subtract *b* from *a*)   ———

   d. Divide by 2 (disregard any remaining fraction)   ———

   e. Add 1 line to find the line on which you will begin to type   ———

3. Figure your horizontal placement by centering your longest line (*keyline*). Set your left margin at the point where you would begin to type this line.

TYPE

4. Type Job 2. Center the main and secondary headings. Begin each line of the body of the copy at the left margin.

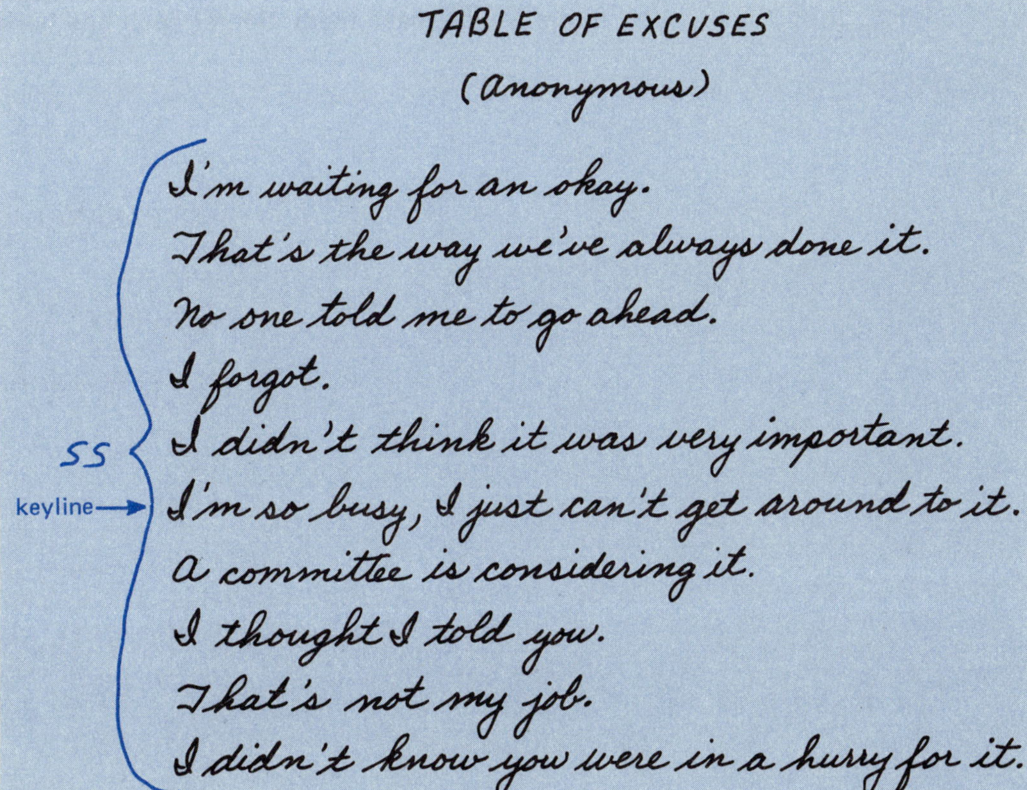

5. Proofread your work and circle any errors you may have made. Use your typing ruler to check your vertical placement. Are your top and bottom margins equal or within one line of being equal?

(turn in for teacher approval)

Half sheet (long side up).

NOTE: In Job 3, you will center an announcement that is in *rough-draft* form. Rough-draft copy has corrections made by hand after it has been typed. These corrections are made with *proofreader's marks*. Each mark represents a change that is to be made in typing the final copy. Study the list of proofreader's marks in the *Appendix*, page 75.

1. Prepare machine for centering.

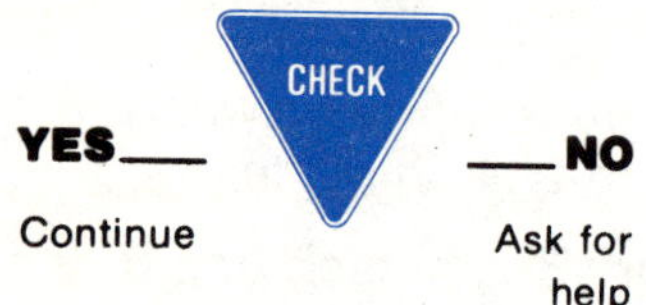

2. Figure your vertical centering, using the spacing directions given in the job. Use the space below to find the line on which you will begin to type the job.

a. ______________

b. ______________

c. ______________

d. ______________

e. ______________

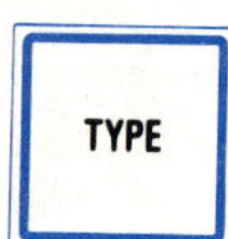

YES____ **CHECK** ____**NO**

Continue   Ask for help

3. Check on page 76 of the *Answer Checkup*. Is your vertical centering correct?

TYPE

4. Type Job 3 after you have looked over the rough-draft corrections. Correct any errors as you make them. Center each line horizontally.

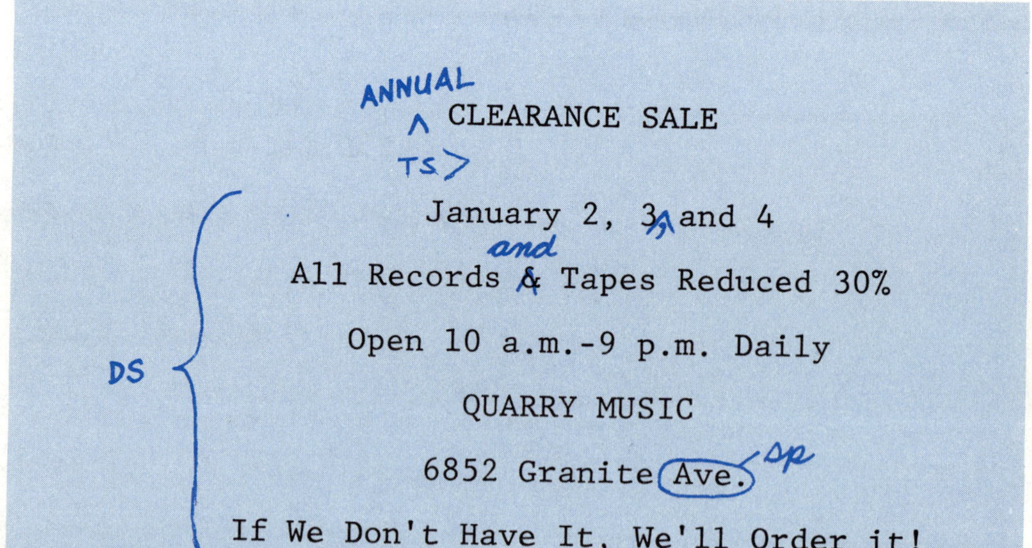

5. Proofread your work to be sure you have corrected all errors.

YES____ **TEACHER APPROVAL** ____**NO**

Continue   Ask for help

6. Use your ruler to check your top and bottom margins. They should be within 1 line of being equal. Check your side margins. Is each line centered horizontally? Turn in this job to your teacher for approval.

To be able to center copy vertically and horizontally on paper of different lengths and widths.

JOB 4   VERTICAL CENTERING ON A FULL SHEET

Full sheet

READ

To center typed material on a full sheet of 11-inch paper, follow the same steps that you did for centering on a half sheet of paper. Since a half sheet has 33 vertical lines, a full sheet has 66 vertical lines. Remember, there are 6 lines to 1 inch:

11 inches
× 6 lines per inch
66 lines on a full sheet.

GET READY

1. Prepare your machine for centering: Clear tabs and margins; insert your paper evenly.

DO

2. Center Job 4 (page 14), both vertically and horizontally on a full sheet of paper. The spacing directions are given in the job. The steps at the right will lead you to the line on which you should begin to type Job 4.

a. Lines on page (11″ × 6 lines/inch) __________

b. Lines needed for job __________

c. Subtract (b) from (a) to find number of blank lines. __________

d. Divide (c) by 2 (drop any remaining fraction) to divide space for margins evenly. __________

e. Add 1 line. This is the line on which you should begin to type Job 4. __________

CHECK

YES____ ____NO

Continue   Ask for help

3. Look on page 76 of your *Answer Checkup.* Is your answer correct?

4. Now, type Job 4.

TYPE

5. Proofread your work and circle any errors you may have made. Measure with your ruler to check your centering. Are your top and bottom margins equal or within one line of being equal? Is each line correctly centered?

PROJECT NO. IV-347

TS >
SS > THE EFFECTS OF IRRIGATION ON THE
SALINITY OF COLORADO RIVER WATER

2"

Dr. Hayato Shinoda
DS > San Diego, CA

2"

DS > April 19--
SS > 21st Century Task Force
Independent Environmental Associates, Inc.
SS > Team IV

Half sheet (short side up)

1. Prepare your typewriter for centering: Clear tabs and margins; set the line-space selector for SS; insert paper (5½″ × 8½″) short side up.

2. Determine the vertical center for Job 5. Leave proper spacing after the headings. SS the body and DS between paragraphs.

   a. Lines available on page (8½″ × 6 lines/inch) ＿＿＿＿＿＿

   b. Lines needed for job (Job 5 is to be typed line-for-line.) ＿＿＿＿＿＿

   c. Subtract (b) from (a) to find lines remaining ＿＿＿＿＿＿

   d. Divide by 2 to find the top margin ＿＿＿＿＿＿

   e. Add 1 and begin to type on Line . . . . ＿＿＿＿＿＿

3. Set your margins for a 40-space line.

   ＿＿＿＿＿＿ Center of paper   ＿＿＿＿＿＿ Center of paper

   −＿＿＿＿＿ Minus ½ the spaces in line   +＿＿＿＿＿ Plus ½ the spaces in line

   ＿＿＿＿＿＿ Left margin   +＿＿＿＿＿ Plus 5 spaces for bell

                                     ＿＿＿＿＿＿ Right margin

   Set a tab stop for a 5-space paragraph indention. Check on page 76 of your *Answer Checkup* to see if your top and side margins are correct.

4. Type Job 5. Proofread and circle any errors you may have missed. Check with your ruler to see if you centered the job correctly.

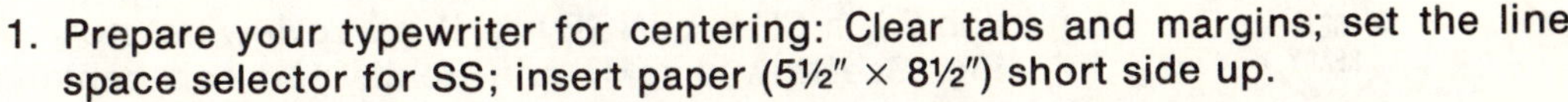

JOB 6 CHALLENGE JOB *(turn in for teacher approval)*

Half sheet (short side up)

Job 6 is a CHALLENGE job. It is a review before you take a test on vertical center-ing. See how quickly and neatly you can center the job vertically. Follow the spacing directions given in the job. Try to complete the job in 20 minutes or less.

1. Prepare your machine for centering and insert your paper short side up.

2. Figure out the horizontal center. Set a tab stop at the center. Set the margins for a 40-space line, in preparation for typing the body of the job. Use the space below to figure your margins.

Left margin = _________   Right margin = _________

3. Figure below the line on which you will begin to type. The announcement is to be typed line-for-line. Therefore, count each line as one line. Remember to count the spaces between, too.

Begin typing on Line _________

4. Type Job 6, following the directions given. Correct errors if you make any. Refer to the proofreader's marks in the *Appendix* if necessary.

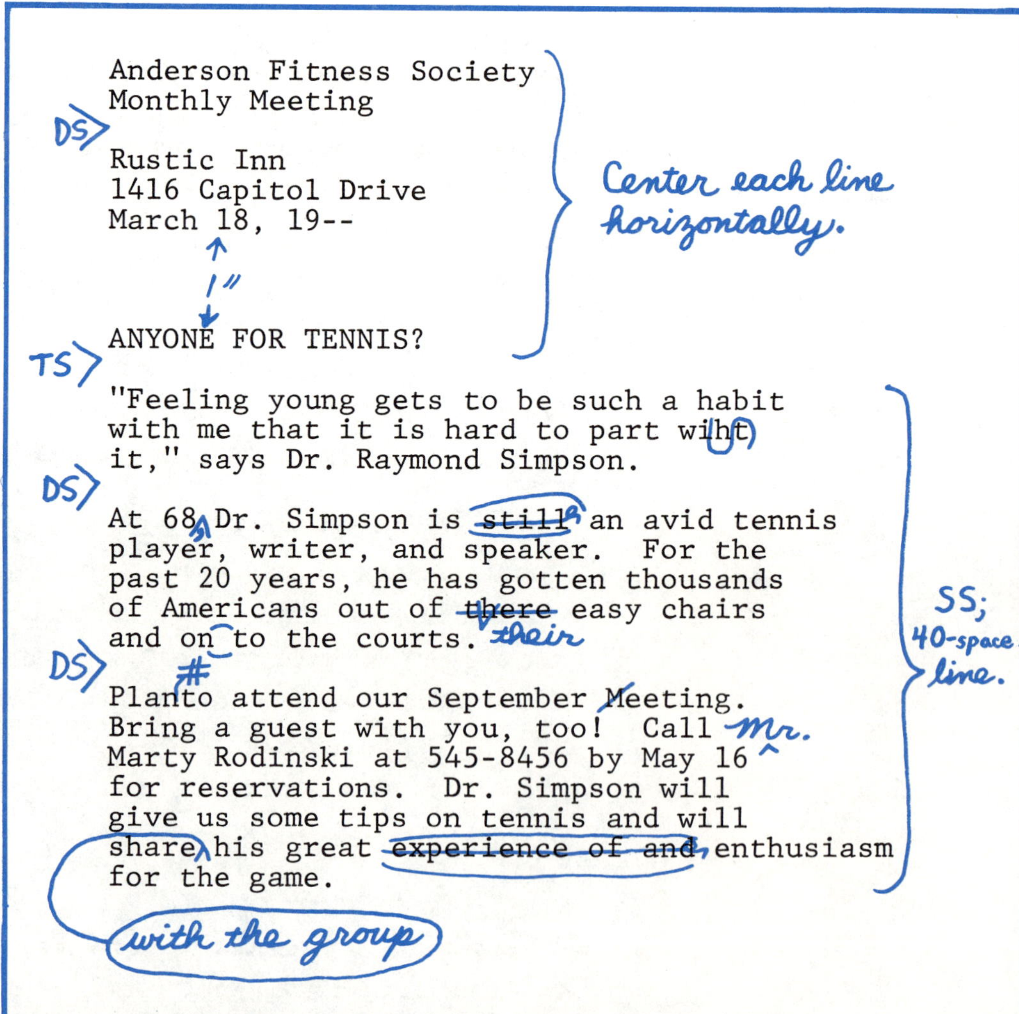

5. Proofread the job when you finish, and correct any errors you may have missed. Check your margins with your ruler. Turn in to your teacher for approval.

Fill in the blanks below.

1. Double-spaced copy has __________ blank line(s) between lines of type.

2. Triple-spaced copy has __________ blank line(s) between lines of type.

3. A main heading with no secondary heading is followed by a
   ______________________ space.

4. Between a main and a secondary heading, you ______________________-
   space.

5. Between a secondary heading and the copy in the job, you
   ______________________ space.

6. Which heading is typed in ALL CAPS, the main or the secondary heading?
   ______________________.

7. Vertical means ______________________ and ______________________.

8. List the 5 steps in vertical centering:

   1 ____

   2 ____

   3 ____

   4 ____

   5 ____

9. There are __________ lines to a vertical inch.

10. To leave a 1″ top margin, you should begin to type on Line __________.

11. There are __________ lines on a half sheet of paper long side up (5½″ long).

12. There are __________ lines on a half sheet of paper short side up (8½″ long).

13. Suppose that you are to type a job which is 11 lines long on a half sheet of
    paper *long side up*. Use the space below to figure the vertical spacing.

    Begin to type on Line __________

14. Suppose that you are to type a job which is 33 lines long on a half sheet of
    paper *short side up*. Use the space below to figure the vertical spacing.

    Begin to type on Line __________

YES______   ______NO

Continue   Ask for
                          help

*Now, check your answers in the Answer Key on page 76. Correct any answers you
may have missed. If you do not understand an answer, ask your teacher for help.*

TEST FOR UNIT 2

Half sheet (short side up)

TYPE

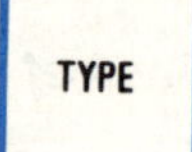

1. Type the announcement shown below on a half sheet short side up. Center the job vertically and center each line horizontally. Follow other directions given on the job. Correct all errors neatly. Try to complete the job in 15 minutes or less.

OUTDOOR LEADERSHIP SEMINAR

Courses Offered Now

TS >

(Dash is 2 hyphens; no space before or after)

DS

June 17 -- July 15

August 9 -- September 11

Training Includes:

Whitewater Rafting

Mountain Backpacking

Outdoor Survival

Contact: Wilderness Guide Institute

303 - 855 - 6048

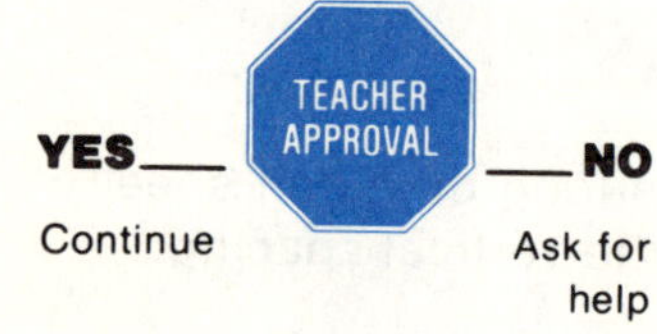

2. When you finish typing, leave your paper in your typewriter. Proofread your work carefully. Correct any errors which you may have missed. Did you finish the announcement in 15 minutes or less?

3. Check your centering with your ruler. Are your top and bottom margins equal or nearly equal?

4. Turn in your test to your teacher.

YES___ TEACHER APPROVAL ___**NO**

Continue — Ask for help

TABLE TYPING, NO COLUMN HEADINGS

When you complete Unit 3, you will be able to type simple tables of 2 to 4 columns with equal space between the columns and equal left and right margins.

PART 1 GOAL

To center columns with equal space between each column.

Up to this point, you have centered a complete line of copy horizontally. Now, you will learn to center *columns* of copy horizontally. The idea is the same—to put half of the line of copy on either side of the center of the paper. The procedure is basically the same: Begin at the center and backspace once for each 2 characters or spaces.

JOB 1   CENTERING GROUPS OF WORDS

Half sheet (long side up)

Center and type the line below by following the steps given.

Backspace	from	this	center	point.

1. From the center of your sheet of paper, backspace 1 space for each 2 letters in the line. If you have a leftover letter at the end of one word, pair it with the first letter of the next word. In this line, you will have the punctuation mark left over. Do not backspace for it.

Backspace from center	BA	CK	SP	AC	EF	RO	MT	HI	SC	EN	·TE	RP	OI	NT	
	1	2	3	4	5	6	7	8	9	10	11	12	13	14	—

2. Backspace 1 space for each 2 spaces between words (8 spaces between words × 4 = 32 spaces ÷ 2 = 16 backspaces).

3. Begin to type where you completed backspacing. Remember to space 8 times after each word.

4. Check to see if the letter *h* in the word *this* is at the center of your paper.

YES____ PROOFREAD/CHECK ____**NO**

Continue · Ask for help

JOB 2 CENTERING COLUMNS OF EQUAL LENGTH

Half sheet (long side up)

READ ➡ Center and type Job 2 horizontally and vertically. DS the job. Leave 8 spaces between each column. After you center and type your heading, follow the steps below to center the columns horizontally.

PREFERRED DIVISION POINTS

what-ever	pro-vided	quan-tity
repub-lic	poli-cies	elec-tric
iden-tify	de-fended	ac-cepted
inter-val	hesi-tate	manu-ally

1. Use the first line as your keyline. Backspace 1 space for each 2 strokes in the columns and for each 2 spaces between the columns (8 spaces × 2 = 16 ÷ 2 = 8 backspaces). Set your left margin where you finish backspacing.

Backspace from center	WH	AT	−E	VE	RP	RO	−V	ID	ED	QU	AN	−T	IT	Y + 16 spaces
	1	2	3	4	5	6	7	8	9	10	11	12	13	+ 8 spaces

2. Space forward 1 space for *each* stroke in *what-ever* and 1 space for *each* of the 8 spaces between Columns 1 and 2. Set your tab stop for Column 2 here. Then space forward 1 space for *each* stroke in *pro-vided* and 1 space for *each* of the 8 spaces between Columns 2 and 3. Set your tab stop for Column 3 here.

TYPE

3. Type Job 2, remembering to tab to the columns as you type. Keep your eyes on your copy as you strike the tab and return keys. Circle any errors you make.

4. Proofread your work when you finish typing. After you take the job from your typewriter, check top, bottom, and side margins to be sure that they are equal or nearly equal.

JOB 3 CENTERING COLUMNS OF EQUAL LENGTH

Half sheet (long side up)

READ ➡ 1. Center Job 3, page 21, vertically and horizontally on a half sheet. DS the job and leave 8 spaces between columns. Use the first line as your keyline. Center and type the heading.

2. Backspace 1 space for each 2 strokes in your keyline (for this job, Line 1).

Backspace from center	AB	SE	NC	EA	BU	ND	AN	CE	AL	IB	IA	BS	OL	UT	E + 24 spaces
	1	2	3	4	5	6	7	8	9	10	11	12	13	14	+ 12 spaces

Set your left margin where you finish backspacing the keyline.

LEARN TO SPELL THESE WORDS

TS

absence	8	abundance	8	alibi	8	absolute
banquet		broadcast		berth		behavior
century		cafeteria		cease		canceled
deceive		detriment		diary		decision
emperor		editorial		elite		emigrant
forfeit		financial		forty		furlough
gesture		guarantee		groan		governor

DS

3. Space forward 1 space for *each* stroke in *absence* and for *each* of the 8 spaces between Columns 1 and 2. Set your tab stop for Column 2. Set your tab stops for Columns 3 and 4 in the same manner. Check on page 76 of your *Answer Checkup* to see if your figures are correct.

4. Type Job 3, keeping your eyes on your copy as you strike the tab and return keys. Proofread your work and circle any errors you may have made.

Read the steps given in the *Guide for Centering Columns* (below). These guides are the same as those which you have followed to do Jobs 1, 2, and 3 in this Unit. You can refer to this *Guide* whenever you need help with the steps for centering columns.

GUIDE FOR CENTERING COLUMNS

1. Clear your margins and tab stops. Find the line on which you will begin to type. Center and type your heading.

2. Find the keyline for horizontal centering purposes. *The keyline is made up of the longest word or phrase in each column, plus the spaces between each column.* The column entries of the keyline usually will not be all on 1 row across, but may jump from row to row across the page.

3. Backspace 1 space for *each 2* strokes in the keyline. If there is a leftover stroke at the end of the keyline, do not count it. Set your left margin where you finish backspacing for the keyline.

4. Set tab stops for each column. Do this by spacing forward 1 space for *each stroke* in the longest item in the first column and 1 space for *each* of the spaces between the 2 columns. Set the tab stop where you finish spacing forward. Repeat this step for additional columns to be typed.

5. Keep your eyes on the copy as you tab to each column and return to the next line. Tab to the next column and continue to type.

To be able to center tables horizontally using the keyline.

JOB 4 TWO-COLUMN TABLE

Half sheet (long side up)

When you center a table horizontally, identify your keyline to figure the widths of the columns correctly. Use the keyline to set your left margin and tab stops.

1. Prepare your machine for centering. Plan your vertical centering for typing Job 4 DS on a half sheet of paper (long side up). Center and type the heading.

2. Center Job 4 horizontally by following the steps given below. Leave 10 spaces between columns.

   a. Identify your keyline:

   Keyline = _________________ + _________________ + 10 spaces
             longest word, Col. 1   longest word, Col. 2 between columns

   b. Backspace 1 space for each 2 strokes in the keyline. Set your left margin where you finish backspacing.

   c. Set your tab stop for Column 2 by spacing forward from the left margin 1 space for *each* stroke in the word *tabulate* and for *each* of the 10 spaces between the 2 columns.

   d. Check page 76 of your *Answer Checkup* to see if your left margin and tab stop are correct.

3. Type Job 4; TS below the heading. DS the table. Keep your eyes on the copy as you tab and return. Proofread your work when you finish and circle any errors.

```
               HOW TO TYPE TABLES


        Space              material

        in                 tables

        by       10 spaces figuring

        where              to

Keyline tabulate           for

        each               column.
```

YES____ | **NO**____
Continue | Ask for help

4. Use your ruler to check your margins. Are they equal or nearly equal? Are there 10 spaces between the words *tabulate* and *for*?

Half sheet (long side up)

1. Prepare your machine for centering. Plan your vertical centering; DS the body of the table. Center and type your main and secondary headings.

2. Center Job 5 horizontally. Leave 10 spaces between columns (10 spaces between Columns 1 and 2 and between Columns 2 and 3 = 20 spaces).

   a. Identify your keyline:

   _________________ + _________________ + _________________ + 20 spaces
   longest item, Col. 1   longest item, Col. 2   longest item, Col. 3

   b. Backspace to center the keyline and set your left margin.

   c. Using your keyline, space forward to set tab stops for Columns 2 and 3.

   d. Check on page 76 of your *Answer Checkup*. Are your left margin and tab stops correct?

3. Type Job 5, double-spacing between lines. Keep your eyes on the copy as you tab and return. Proofread when you finish typing and circle any errors.

ANIMALS AND THEIR YOUNG

(With Names of Groups)

swan	cygnet	bevy of swans
duck	duckling	brace of ducks
cat	kitten	clowder of cats
kangaroo	joey	mob of kangaroos
goose	gosling	gaggle of geese
fox	kit	leash of foxes
hare	leveret	down of hares
hound	whelp	cry of hounds

4. Check with your ruler. Are your margins equal or nearly equal? Is your spacing equal between the longest items in the columns?

JOB 6 ALIGNING FIGURES

Half sheet (long side up)

When a column has numbers of different lengths, align them to the right (at the "ones" column). Set a tab stop for each column at the point where you will need to space forward or backspace the least. In the example at the right, most of the numbers in Column 2 have 3 digits. Set a tab at the point where you would type these 3-digit numbers and then space forward or backspace to align the shorter or longer numbers in the column.

Type Job 6 (below) following these steps. DS the table and leave 10 spaces between columns.

Example

left margin ↓	tab ↓
326	762
10	216
411	2,318
8	148
124	32
75	8,957
893	631

1. Center the table vertically on a half sheet.

2. Identify your keyline. Leave 10 spaces between columns. Backspace to center the keyline and set your left margin.

3. Space forward 1 space for *each* stroke in the first column entry and 1 space for *each* of the 10 spaces between Columns 1 and 2.

    * This brings you to the point where you will begin to type 3-digit numbers in Column 2. Since all but 1 of the numbers in this column are 3-digit numbers, set your tab stop here.

4. Space forward a space for *each* stroke in the second column entry and 1 space for *each* of the 10 spaces between between Columns 2 and 3.

    * This brings you to the point where you will begin to type the longest number in Column 3, *8,642*. But the other numbers in Column 3 are 3-digit numbers. So space forward 2 spaces and set your tab stop for Column 3. Remember to backspace 2 spaces before you type 8,642.

5. Set a tab stop for Column 4, using the same method you used in Steps 3 and 4.

1,503	713	8,642	928
4,728	259	301	1,630
642	18	157	375
3,907	145	614	842

6. Proofread and circle any errors you may have made. Use your typing ruler to check: Are there 10 spaces between the *longest* numbers in each column?

JOB 7   ALIGNING AMOUNTS OF MONEY

Half sheet (long side up)

When a column lists amounts of money, type a dollar sign before the first amount. If a total is given, underline the last amount before you type the total. The line should be as long as the longest amount in the column (including the dollar sign). DS below the underline. Type another dollar sign before the total.

$148	$253	$136
165	416	429
30	107	205
279	194	87
DS __254__	__28__	__118__
$876	$998	$975

Type the simple table to practice typing amounts of money in columns.

1. Plan your vertical centering for DS copy on a half sheet of paper.

2. Find your keyline and plan your horizontal centering. Leave 12 spaces between each column.

3. Set your left margin and tab stops. Remember to set each tab stop at the point which will require the least spacing forward or backspacing.

4. Proofread and circle your errors. Check the spacing and margins. Are there 12 spaces between the columns?

JOB 8   TYPING A TABLE WITH AMOUNTS OF MONEY

Half sheet (long side up)

Align dollar signs 1 space to the left of the *longest* amount in a column. The longest amount often is the total. So, plan ahead when you type the first dollar sign to allow for the total.

Example

$ 5,319,208	$ 986
72,663,451	72
11,794,823	4,163
7,902,010	505
__3,371,568__	__239__
$101,051,060	$5,965

1. Plan your vertical centering for typing Job 8 (page 26) on a half sheet. DS the body. Type the table heading.

2. Find your keyline and plan your horizontal centering. Leave 12 spaces between columns. Set the left margin and tab stop. Remember to set the tab at the point which will require the least spacing forward or backspacing.

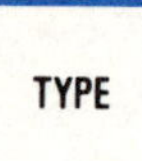

3. Type the table. Remember to align the dollar signs. Proofread your work when you finish and circle any errors.

COMPONENTS OF THE BUDGET

Housing costs	$5,400
Clothing expenses	3,500
Food	2,900
Medical costs	750
Household expenses	2,400
Total	$14,950

JOB 9 CHALLENGE JOB *(turn in for teacher approval)*

Half sheet (long side up)

Job 9 is a CHALLENGE job. It is a review before you take a test on centering columns in a table. Try to finish within 15 minutes.

1. Plan your vertical and horizontal centering. Use proper spacing after the main and secondary headings. SS the table and leave 8 spaces between columns. Use your keyline to plan your horizontal centering of the columns. Correct errors.

MAJOR LEAGUE BASEBALL

(All-Time Records)

Consecutive games played	Lou Gehrig	2,130
Season runs batted in	Hack Wilson	190
Career base hits	Ty Cobb	4,191
Lifetime runs batted in	Hank Aaron	2,297
Consecutive game hits	Joe Di Maggio	56
Season base hits	George Sisler	257
Lifetime steals home	Ty Cobb	35
Lifetime home runs	Hank Aaron	755
Lifetime stolen bases	Lou Brock	938

YES_____ _____NO

Continue   Ask for
                  help

2. Proofread the job when you finish, and correct any errors you may have missed. Check your margins with your ruler. Turn in Job 9 to your teacher for approval.

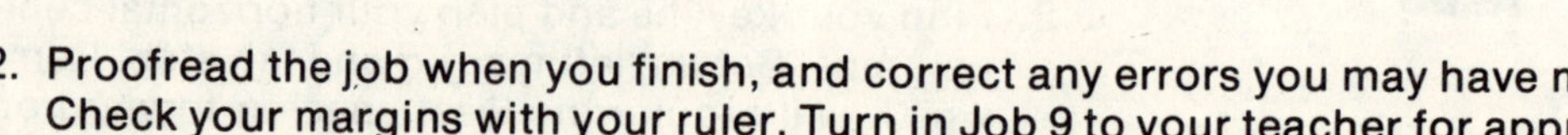

Fill in the blanks.

1. There are ________ lines per vertical inch on both pica and elite typewriters.

2. If you have a table to type which will use 37 lines of your *full* sheet of paper (8½ × 11″), on what line would you begin to type?

   Begin typing on Line ________.

3. If you have a table to type which will use 15 lines of your *half* sheet of paper, long side up (8½ × 5½″), on what line would you begin to type?

   Begin typing on Line ________.

4. To center columns of unequal length horizontally, use the keyline, which is made up of the ________________________ word or phrase in each column and the spaces between columns.

5. After backspacing for the words or phrases in the keyline, continue to backspace for the spaces to be left between ________________________.

6. Using the backspace-from-center method for centering a table, set the ________________________ margin where you complete backspacing the keyline.

7. After you have set the left margin for a table, set your tab stops for each column by spacing forward ________ space(s) for each stroke and ________ space(s) for each space between the columns.

8. Suppose that you want to set a tab stop for a column which has *whole* numbers of different lengths. Should you align the column at the left or at the right?

   ____

9. When you type a column with numbers, set a tab stop at the point which requires the least spacing forward or backspacing. For the column shown below, set your tab stop at which space (circle one)?   A   B   C

<pre>
      A B   C
   $ 963.17
       85.08
    1,426.33
      769.20
       29.50
      231.75
      548.41
      ____

   $4,053.44
</pre>

Now, check your answer in the Answer Checkup on page 76. Correct any answers you may have missed. If you do not understand an answer, ask your teacher for help.

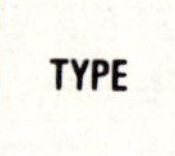

TEST ON UNIT 3

Full sheet

1. Type the table below on a full sheet of paper. Plan your vertical centering, following correct spacing guides for typing the main and secondary headings and double-spacing the rest of the table. Type the headings.

2. Find the keyline and plan your horizontal centering. When you set your tab stop for Column 3, remember to plan ahead and use correct spacing for the *longest* amount in the column.

3. Type the table, correcting any errors as you make them. Try to finish in 20 minutes or less.

REAL ESTATE SALES OF TOP FIFTEEN REPRESENTATIVES
(By Volume of Sales)
(In Rank Order)

Magdalena Santiago	Kingsbury Realty	$ 16,568,200
Diane Hilliard	Glen Oaks Realty	13,432,050
Ricardo DeAyora	Freschie & Associates	12,326,900
Silvia Wilfredo	Loma Realty	9,967,800
Toshi Shinoba	Coast West Realty	9,272,400
Wes Wisley	Lincoln Real Estate	8,346,000
Charles Wheelock	Lakeside Realty	8,168,300
Tien Chang	Forrest Realty	7,172,800
Porter Thompson	Classical Properties	6,079,600
Nestor Jimenez	Ellis Realty	4,987,300
Julia Sayama	Win-Code Realtors	1,942,500
Xiomara Melendez	Associated Brokers Service	876,100
Elizabeth Maxwell	Cantieri Realty	743,900
Nate Roberts	Baxter and Associates	332,600
Sharon Larsen	Rodriguez and Associates	99,300
Total		$100,271,200

4. When you finish typing, leave your paper in your typewriter. Proofread your work carefully. Correct any errors which you may have overlooked as you typed.

5. Check your centering with your ruler. Are your margins equal or nearly equal? Are there 6 spaces between the *longest* items in each column? Is the word *Total* indented 3 spaces from the left margin? Did you finish the job in 20 minutes?

6. Turn in your test to your teacher.

Unit 3 Test

4

TABLES WITH COLUMN HEADINGS

When you complete Unit 4, you will be able to center and type tables with column headings over the columns.

PART 1 GOAL

To center a shorter column heading over a column in a table.

READ

Most tables have headings over the columns. When the *columns* are longer than the headings, the headings are centered over the columns. When the *headings* are longer than the columns, the columns are centered under the headings.

Example

```
           UNITED STATES' LARGEST BUILDINGS


           Col. A                    Col. B
           Building                  Stories

           Sears Tower                 110
           World Trade Center          110
           Empire State                102
           Standard Oil                 80
           John Hancock Center         100
```

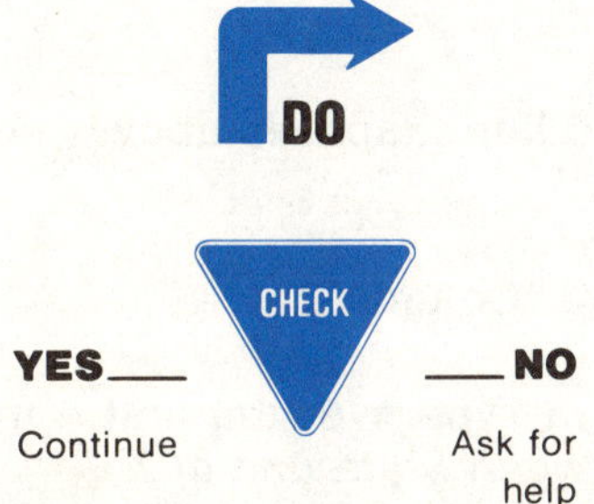
DO

Look at the example above.

In which column is the heading centered over the column? ______________

In which column is the column centered under the heading? ______________

Compare your answers with the *Answer Checkup*, page 76.

CHECK

YES___ ___NO

Continue   Ask for help

GUIDES FOR CENTERING A HEADING OVER A COLUMN

To center a column heading which is *shorter* than the items in the column:

1. Plan your vertical and horizontal centering as usual. Set your left margin and tab stops.

2. From the left margin or tab stop, find the center of the column. Do this by spacing forward 1 space for each 2 characters or spaces in the longest item in the column.

3. Backspace 1 space for each 2 characters or spaces in the heading. Type the heading and underscore it.

Half sheet (long side up)

	Type	Example
Drill 1	Peninsula	State of Florida

	Month	Stone
Drill 2	December	Turquoise

	Extreme	Location
Drill 3	Highest temperature	Death Valley

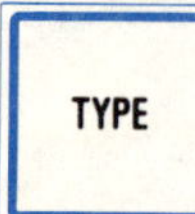

1. Beginning on Line 9, center and type the keyline, leaving 6 spaces between columns.

Backspace from center

Pe	ni	ns	ul	aS	ta	te	#o	f#	Fl	or	id	a	12	34	56
1	2	3	4	5	6	7	8	9	10	11	12	–	13	14	15

Set your left margin. Space forward 1 stroke for each letter in *Peninsula* and for your spaces between columns. Set a tab for Column 2.

2. Find the center of the first column.

Space forward

Pe	ni	ns	ul	a
1	2	3	4	– spaces

3. Backspace to center the heading over the column.

Backspace

Ty	pe
1	2 spaces

4. Roll platen back *2* lines so that you will type on the line 2 spaces above the column. Type the heading and underscore it.

5. Repeat these steps to center the second heading over Column 2.

Check to see if you centered Drill 1 correctly. Is the *T* in *Type* over the first *n* in Pe*n*insula? Is the first *E* in *Example* over the space between *State* and *of*?

Space down 7 lines to center and type the keyline of Drill 2. Follow the steps given for Drill 1 to center the headings for Drill 2. Leave 6 spaces between columns.

TYPE

Follow the same steps to complete Drill 3, spacing down 7 lines to center and type the keyline of Drill 3. Leave 6 spaces between the columns.

Check page 76 of the *Answer Checkup* to see if your column headings for Drills 2 and 3 begin at the correct spaces.

Half sheet (long side up)

When a table has column headings, DS between the heading and the first line of the column. The spacing after the main and secondary headings remains the same.

1. Prepare your machine for centering. Plan your vertical centering; DS the columns. Center and type your main and secondary headings.

2. Plan your horizontal centering using your keyline (shown in color, below). Leave 10 spaces between the columns. Set your left margin where you completed backspacing.

   Left margin = ————

3. Set the tab stop for Column 2. Space forward 1 space for each stroke in *Labrador Retriever* and for the 10 spaces between Columns 1 and 2.

   Tab stop for Column 2 = ————

4. Center the heading *Sporting* over the longest line in Column 1. From the left margin, space forward 1 space for every 2 strokes in *Labrador Retriever*. Then, backspace 1 space for every 2 strokes in the heading *Sporting*.

   Begin to type *Sporting* at Space ————.

5. Follow the same steps to center the heading *Hounds* over Column 2.

   Begin to type *Hounds* at Space ————.

6. Check page 76 in your *Answer Checkup* to see if your figures are correct. Then, type Job 2.

DOGS BRED FOR HUNTING

(By Class)

Sporting		Hounds
Golden Retriever		Afghan
Labrador Retriever	10	Greyhound
German Short Hair		Basset
Pointer		Beagle
Irish Setter		Bloodhound
English Spaniel		Foxhound

7. Proofread your work and circle any errors you may have made.

Full sheet

1. Prepare machine for centering. Plan the vertical centering; DS the columns. Center and type the main and secondary headings.

2. Plan horizontal centering using your keyline. Leave 8 spaces between the columns. Set the left margin where you completed backspacing. Space forward and set tab stops for each column.

3. Center and type the three column headings over the columns. Remember to underscore the column headings. See page 29 for help if necessary.

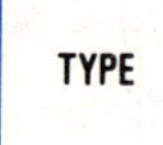

4. Type the rest of the job, correcting any errors you may make.

SOME EARLY INDIAN TRIBES

United States and Canada

Tribe	Culture	Early Locality
Arapaho	Plains	Colorado, Nebraska
Cheyenne	Plains	Minnesota, Dakotas
Comanche	Plains	Texas, Oklahoma
Creek	S.E. Woodland	Georgia, Alabama
Huron	E. Woodland	Ontario
Kiowa	Plains	Colorado, Kansas
Kwakiutl	N.W. Pacific	British Columbia
Menominee	N. Woodland	Wisconsin
Navajo	S.W. Desert	New Mexico, Arizona
Pawnee	Plains	Kansas, Nebraska
Timucua	E. Woodland	Florida
Tsimshian	N.W. Pacific	British Columbia

5. Proofread your work to be sure it is correct. Check your spacing. Are there 8 spaces between *Menominee* and Column 2 and between *S. E. Woodland* and Column 3? Are your margins equal or nearly equal? Turn the job in for approval.

To be able to type tables with column headings longer than the column entries.

JOB 4 CENTERING SHORT COLUMNS UNDER LONGER HEADINGS

Half sheet (long side up)

When headings in a table are longer than the column entries, the headings make up the keyline. The column entries are centered under the headings.

1. Prepare your machine for centering; space down to Line 11 on a half sheet of paper.

2. Center and type Drill 1 (below), following these steps:

   a. Backspace to center the keyline, *Type of InvestmentPercent of Total.* Leave 10 spaces between columns. Type and underscore the column headings.

   b. DS after you type the headings. From the beginning of the heading in Column 1, space forward 1 space for each 2 spaces in the heading. This brings you to the center of Column 1. Backspace 1 space for each 2 strokes in the column entry *Life Insurance.* Type *Life Insurance* where you finish backspacing. Follow the same steps to type *14* in Column 2.

Drill 1

Type of Investment	Percent of Total
Life Insurance	14

Drill 2

Regional Office	Increase
Chicago	1.4%

3. Center and type Drill 2 as you did Drill 1. Leave 10 spaces between columns.

Follow the steps given in the *Guide* below whenever you center a heading over a column in a table.

GUIDES FOR CENTERING A COLUMN UNDER A HEADING

To center a column heading which is *longer* than the entries in the column:

1. Plan your vertical centering as usual.

2. Find the left margin by backspacing for the keyline. Use the heading as part of the keyline when the heading is the longest item in the column. Type column headings and underscore them. DS after the column headings.

3. From the beginning of the heading, space forward 1 space for each 2 strokes or spaces in the heading. You are now at the center of the heading.

4. From the center of the heading, backspace 1 space for each 2 strokes or spaces in the longest item in the column. Set your tab stop here and type all items in the column beginning at this point.

Half sheet (long side up)

Follow the steps below to center and type Job 5. Refer to the *Guide* on page 33 if you need help with the steps for centering columns under longer headings.

1. Plan your vertical centering; DS the body of the table (remember to DS below a column heading). Center and type the main and secondary headings.

2. Center the keyline (3 column headings plus 8 spaces between each column). Set your left margin and tab stops for the headings. You will need to reset these later to type the body of the table. Type and underscore the column headings.

3. Center the longest entry in each column under the column heading.

   a. From the beginning of the column heading, space forward 1 space for each 2 strokes in the column heading. This brings you to the column's center.

   b. Backspace 1 space for each 2 strokes in the longest entry in the column. Reset your tab stop (or your left margin for the first column) at this point.

4. Type the rest of the table, remembering to DS after the column headings.

SELECTED AIR CARRIERS

(Based in the U.S.)

Code	Certified Air Carrier	Home Office Location
DL	Delta	Atlanta
EA	Eastern	Miami
FL	Frontier	Denver
OZ	Ozark	St. Louis
UA	United	Chicago
WA	Western	Salt Lake City
WO	World Airways	Oakland

YES______ ______NO

Continue   Ask for
                  help

5. Proofread and circle any errors. Use your typing ruler to check the job for correct spacing. Are your margins equal or nearly equal? Are the columns placed so that the longest item in each column is centered under the column heading?

(Turn in for teacher approval)

Half sheet (long side up)

Center Job 6 vertically and horizontally on a half sheet of paper, following the steps given below. Correct any errors you make as you type.

1. Plan your vertical centering for DS copy. Center and type the main and secondary headings.

2. Center, type, and underscore the column headings. Leave 4 spaces between each heading.

3. Center the longest column entry under each column heading. Reset the left margin and 3 tab stops. Remember to set the tab stop for Column 4 at the point which will require the least spacing forward and backspacing. The longest column entry in each column is highlighted.

4. Type the column entries. Indent the last item in Column 1, *Total*, 5 spaces from the left margin.

<u>Cache National Forest</u>

Fourth 4th Quarter Collections

<u>Date Reported</u>	Responsible Party	Campground	<u>Amt.</u> Collected
October 2 (9)	~~Chuck~~ *Charles* Lutz	Senneca	$12,268.22
October 18	Gail Brostrom	Giunavah	10,237.64
October 28 (20)	~~Carl~~ *Carmen* Reyes	Unitah	8,721.89
October 29	*Julia Izumi*	Summit	7,546.01
November 16	Mike Potter	Beaver	~~4,826.14~~ *5,322.64*
December 8	Niel Roberts	Otter	4,826.14
Total			~~$48,426.04~~ *48,958.54*

5. Proofread your work again. Correct any errors which you may have overlooked. Then, use your ruler to check your spacing and margins. Are all parts of the job centered correctly? Turn the job in for approval.

To be able to type tables with short and long headings.

Up to now, you have centered tables with column headings which were either all shorter or all longer than the columns under them. In most tables, there are both shorter and longer headings over the columns. In Part 3, you will learn to type tables with this more common mixture of shorter and longer column headings.

JOB 7 CENTERING TABLES WITH MIXED-LENGTH COLUMN HEADINGS

Half sheet (long side up)

A keyline, as you know, may skip from a column heading to a column entry and back to a column heading. Center and type Drill 1 and Drill 2, following the steps given below and on page 37.

Drill 1

<u>Title of Poem</u>		<u>Author</u>
If	12	Rudyard Kipling
Trees		Joyce Kilmer

1. Space down to Line 10 on a half sheet of paper.

2. Center the keyline (*Title of Poem Rudyard Kipling + 12 spaces*). Set the left margin. Type the heading for Column 1 and underscore it.

3. Space forward 1 space for each of the 12 spaces between the columns. This brings you to the point where you will type the longest item in Column 2. Set a tab stop here.

4. Type the column heading for Column 2 by following these steps:

   a. Space forward 1 space for each 2 strokes in *Rudyard Kipling*. This brings you to the center of the longest item in Column 2.

   b. Backspace 1 space for each 2 strokes in the column heading (*Author*). At the point where you finish backspacing, type the heading and underscore it.

5. DS, then reset the left margin for typing the entries in Column 1 by following these steps:

   a. Space forward 1 space for each 2 strokes in the column heading (*Title of Poem*). This brings you to the center of the longest item in Column 1.

   b. Backspace 1 space for each 2 strokes in the longest column entry (*Trees*). At the point where you finish backspacing, set your left margin again. Type the column entries for Column 1 from this point.

6. Type the rest of Drill 1.

Animal Name	Male	Female	Young
Deer	Buck	Doe	Fawn
Cattle	Bull	Cow	Calf
Horse	Stallion	Mare	Foal

1. Space down 7 lines from the line where you finished typing Drill 1.

2. Find your keyline for Drill 2. Leave 6 spaces between the longest items in each column. Fill in the spaces below to shown your keyline for Drill 2.

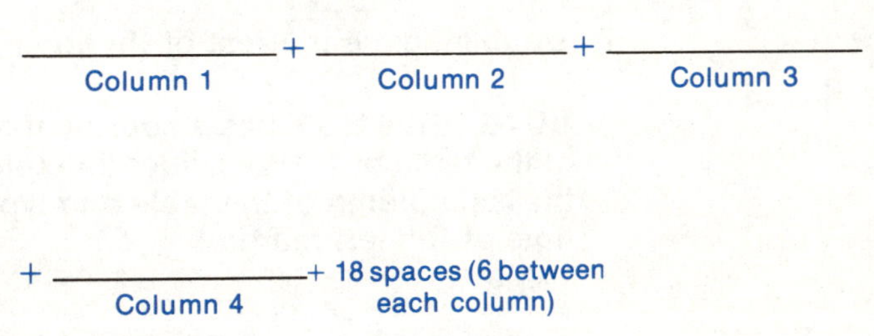

Are the keyline answers correct? Check the *Answer Checkup*, page 77.

3. Center the keyline and set your left margin at the point where you finish backspacing. Type the heading for Column 1 (*Animal Name*) and underscore it.

4. Set your tab stops for Columns 2, 3, and 4. Space forward 1 space for each of the 6 spaces between the *longest* items in each column and set the tabs.

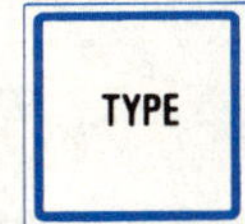

5. Type and underscore the column headings for Columns 2, 3, and 4 by tabbing to the points where you should begin typing the longest items in these columns.

   a. If the column heading is the *longest* item in the column, type the heading. Then center the longest column entry *under* the heading and reset your tab stop.

   b. If the column heading is *shorter* than the longest item in the column, find the center of the longest item and center the column heading *over* the column. Leave the tab stop where it is and type the column items from this point.

6. DS, then reset your left margin for typing the entries in Column 1 by centering the longest column entry under the heading. See 5 (a).

7. Proofread and circle any errors. Check to see that you have the correct number of spaces between the columns (12 spaces for Drill 1 and 6 spaces for Drill 2).

JOB 8   THREE-COLUMN TABLE WITH MIXED HEADINGS

Full sheet

1. Plan your vertical centering (DS the column entries; SS the 2-line main heading). Type the main and secondary headings. Then TS.

2. Center the keyline, leaving 4 spaces between each column. Set your left margin at the point where you finished backspacing for the keyline.

3. Set the tab stops for Columns 2 and 3 by spacing forward 1 space for each stroke in the keyline.

4. Center and type the headings for Columns 1 and 2 over the columns. Tab to Column 3 and begin the heading at the tab stop.

5. Reset the tab stop for Column 3. Center the longest entry in the column under the heading. Remember to set the tab at the point which requires the least spacing forward or backspacing and to align the dollar signs.

YES___ ___**NO**

Continue   Ask for
                        help

6. Check on page 77 of your *Answer Checkup*. Are the margin and tab stops correct?

7. Double-space the rest of the job.

NOTE: This table has a source note. The note is separated from the last line of the table by a 1½" divider line (pica, 15 strokes; elite, 18 strokes). SS below the last column of the table and type the 1½" line; then DS to type the source note at the left margin.

LAKEWOOD TERRACE, INC. INCIDENTAL APARTMENT EXPENSES May 1, – May 31, 19--		
Place Purchased	*Purpose*	*Total Amount*
Builder's Center	Panel bedroom	$ 162.38
The Paint Company	Paint kitchen	85.82
Alpine Pest Control	Spray lawn	37.82
Grand Central	Replace lightbulbs	8.46
S and B Plumbing	Fix faucets	53.81
Jerry's Appliances	Repair dryer	79.95
Glenn's Roofing	Repair roof	62.43
Universal Sprinkler	Replace sprinkler	23.68
Total		$ 514.35

SOURCE: Lakewood Terrace, Inc., Income Statement.

YES___ ___**NO**

Continue   Ask for
                        help

8. Proofread thnd circle any errors. Using your ruler, check to see if there are 12 spaces between the headings of Columns 1 and 2 and 9 spaces between the headings of Columns 2 and 3. Are your dollar signs aligned?

JOB 9 FOUR-COLUMN TABLE WITH MIXED HEADINGS

Half sheet (long side up)

DO

1. Center Job 9 vertically on a half sheet of paper; DS the column entries. Center and type the main and secondary headings.

2. Find your keyline, leaving 4 spaces between columns. Center the keyline and set the left margin.

3. Set the tab stops for Columns 2, 3, and 4 by spacing forward from the left margin 1 space for each stroke of the keyline. Type and underscore the heading for Column 4.

4. Center, type, and underscore the headings for Columns 1, 2, and 3 over their columns.

5. Center the longest item in Column 4 under the column heading and reset your tab stop for this column. Be sure that you align the + and − signs as you would align $ signs in a column.

   NOTE: This table contains numbers with fractions. Line up the whole numbers when you type columns with fractions. Space once between the whole number and the fraction, and use a diagonal in the fraction.

CHECK

YES____ ____NO

Continue   Ask for help

TYPE

6. At what space will you begin to type the entries for Column 1? _______ For Column 2? _______ For Column 3? _______ For Column 4? _______ Look on page 77 of your *Answer Checkup* to see if your figures are correct.

7. Double-space the rest of Job 9.

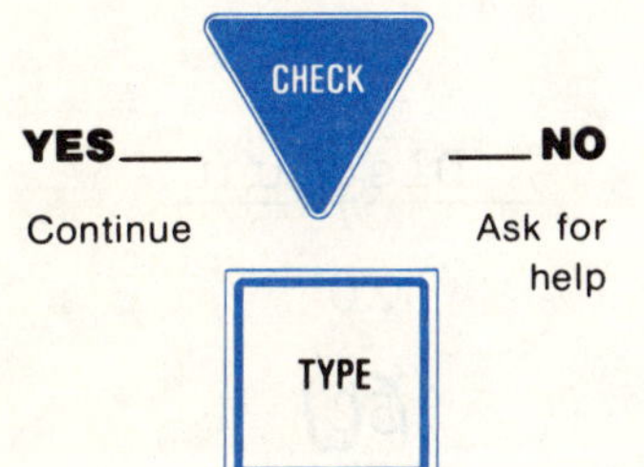

PORTFOLIO OF
~~SELECTED~~ ENERGY STOCKS

Percent Change During Last ⑥ Months

Stock	Begin	End	Percent Change
Tri-State Energy	5 3/4	7 1/8	+ 6.25
High Country Oil and Gas	1 3/8	2 15/16	+ 45.45
Universal Energy	4 1/2	9	+100.00
Wyoming Natural Gas	3 3/4	2 1/2	− 33.33
Double Eagle Solar	10 11/16	11 3/4	+ 21.43
McFarland Oils	14 1/4	13 1/4	− 7.02
Tiepe ~~Fuel~~ Oil Corporation	5 1/8	6 1/8	+ 20.00

YES____ ____NO

Continue   Ask for help

8. Proofread and circle any errors you may have made. Use your ruler to check your margins and spacing between columns. Are there 6 spaces between the longest items in each column? Are your fractions aligned?

Full sheet

Job 10 is a CHALLENGE job which you will turn in for approval when you finish. Try to complete the job in 25 minutes or less.

1. Center Job 10 vertically; DS the column entries. Center and type the main and secondary headings.

2. Center your keyline, leaving 4 spaces between the longest items in the columns. Remember that the dollar signs align one space to the left of the largest amount in the column.

3. Type Job 10, correcting any errors you make as you work.

THE POWER GOLF COMPANY'S SALE ITEMS

Summer, 19--

Item ~~Product~~	Retail Price	Sale Price	% Discount
Utility Golf Club	$ 35.00	$ 28.00	20
Club G*u*ard Bag	150.00	112.50	52
Golden Golf Gloves	10.95	7.66	30
Deluxe Ball Retriever	*22.00*	*16.50*	*25*
Ultraflight Shoes	40.00	36.40	9
Plastic Golf Tubes	.80	.40	50
Golf Bag Travel Cover	20.95	16.76	20
Colorful Cl*u*ob Cover	5.00	3.50	30
Rugged Golf Cart	*79.00*	*47.40*	*40*
golf Cap	10.95	9.85	10

4. Before you take your paper from the machine, proofread your work again. Correct any errors you may have missed. Use your ruler to check your centering and spacing. Are your periods aligned? Did you finish in 25 minutes or less? Turn in Job 10 for approval.

Answer the following questions.

1. When a column is (circle one) *longer/shorter* than the column heading, center the heading over the column.

2. When a column is (circle one) *longer/shorter* than the column heading, center the column under the heading.

3. When a table has column headings, _______________________-space after the main heading before typing the column headings.

4. When a table has column headings, _______________________-space after the column headings before typing the body of the table.

5. When all of the headings in a table are (circle one) *longer/shorter* than the column entries, the headings make up the keyline.

6. When the column heading is longer than the entries in the column, find the center of the column by spacing forward from the beginning of the heading __________ space(s) for every __________ stroke(s) in the heading.

7. To center a column under the column heading, from the center of the heading backspace __________ space(s) for every __________ stroke(s) in the longest entry in the column.

8. To type a 1½″ line on a PICA typewriter, strike the underscore key __________ times (10 strokes/inch × 1½″).

9. To type a 1½″ line on an ELITE typewriter, strike the underscore key __________ times (12 strokes/inch × 1½″).

10. To type the 1½″ divider line between the last line of copy in a table and the source note, _______________________-space from the last line of the table.

11. To type the source note, _______________________-space below the 1½″ divider line.

12. Leave __________ space(s) between a whole number and a fraction.

13. In a column with whole numbers and fractions, where do you align the column (circle one)? *At the left edge / at the "ones" column of the whole numbers / at the right.*

14. In a column with amounts of money, the dollar signs are aligned to the left of the _______________________ amount of money in the column.

15. Figures with decimals should be aligned (circle one) *at the left / at the decimal point / at the right.*

Check on page 77 of your Answer Checkup to see if you have answered these questions correctly. If you do not understand an answer, ask your teacher for help.

Full Sheet

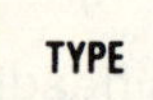

1. Center the table below both vertically and horizontally. DS the body of the table and leave 4 spaces between each column.

2. Try to complete the job in 25 minutes or less. Correct any errors you make as you type.

PENROSE HIGH SCHOOL CRAFT FAIR

Net Profit

Project	Units Sold	Unit Price	Profit
Woven place mat	36	$1.42	$51.12
Linen napkin	28	1.05	29.40
Art candle	11	2.36	25.96
Wooden napkin ring	16	.87	13.92
Wooden cheese board	7	10.29	72.03
Raku pot	15	6.08	91.20
Coffee mug	9	1.54	13.86
Small bowl	17	2.19	37.23
Large bowl	6	5.76	34.56
Teapot	4	10.51	42.04
Total			$411.32

YES ___ ___ **NO**

Continue   Ask for help

3. Proofread your work again to be sure that you have corrected any errors you may have made. Use your ruler to check your margins and spacing. Turn the job in for approval.

UNRULED FORMS

When you complete Unit 5, you will be able to type file folder labels, employee convention badges, postal cards, and address cards.

JOB 1 TYPING FILE FOLDER LABELS

Form 2, page 121

Labels are placed on file folders to show what information is filed in the folder. The folders in the illustration below have a tab. The typed label is attached to the tab. You can reuse a file folder by typing a new label and placing it over the old label. Labels are not centered. Rather, you type the information near the top left corner so that the folders are easy to read.

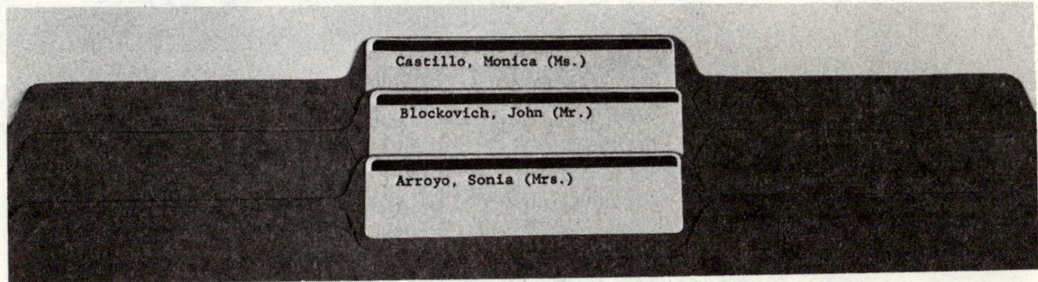

Labels are self-adhesive. They come attached to a waxed backing sheet. After you type a label, peel it off of the sheet and attach it to the tab on the folder. To type this kind of label, follow these steps:

1. Insert the strip of labels into the typewriter.

2. Begin typing on Line 2, 3 spaces from the left edge.

3. List names index-style: Last name, first name, middle initial, and in parentheses personal title (Mr., Miss, Mrs., Ms.). List company names in the usual order. This allows you to file folders easily in alphabetical order.

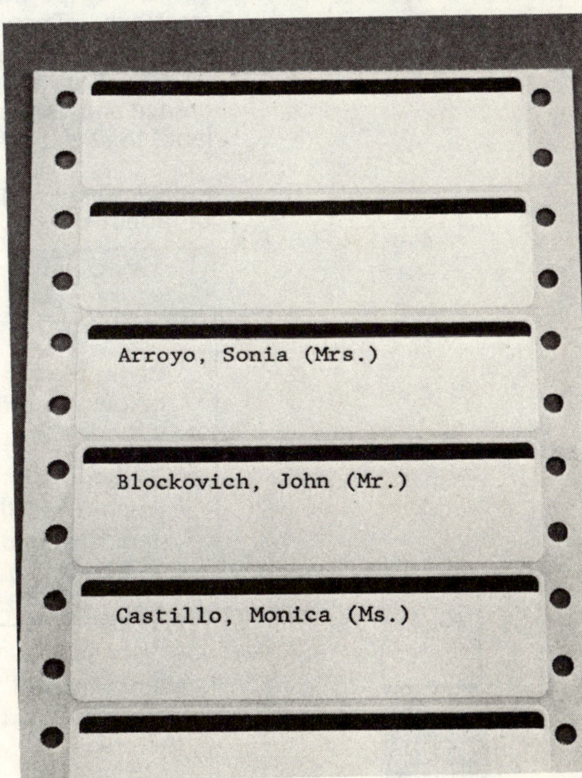

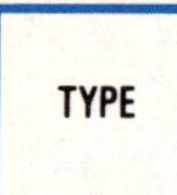

1. Insert Form 2 and space down to Line 2. Be sure the labels are straight. If necessary, use the variable line spacer to adjust. Set left margin 3 spaces from the left edge of the labels.

2. Type the labels for the 9 names given below. Proofread and circle errors.

Arroyo, Sonia (Mrs.)	Vasquez, Charles (Dr.)	Saulnier, Donald (Mr.)
Blockovich, John (Mr.)	Tanaka, H. C. (Mr.)	Pioneer Auto Co.
Castillo, Monica (Ms.)	Page, Sandra (Professor)	Kuhn Sheet Metal

JOB 2   TYPING HANGING FOLDER LABELS

Form 3, page 121

A hanging folder has a clear plastic slot to hold a label. After typing the label, fold it and slip it into the clear slot. A hanging folder can be used again and again. Simply replace the typed label with a new label.

The labels used for hanging folders come in strips with creases and perforations. The perforation lines show you where to separate the labels after they are typed. The crease shows you where to fold the label to slip it into the slot.

Follow these steps to type this kind of label:

1. Insert the strip of labels into your typewriter. Be sure it is in straight.

2. Begin to type on the line right below the crease, close to the left edge.

3. Type names in index order, as you did for file folder labels in Job 1. Because the labels are not wide enough, do not include the title.

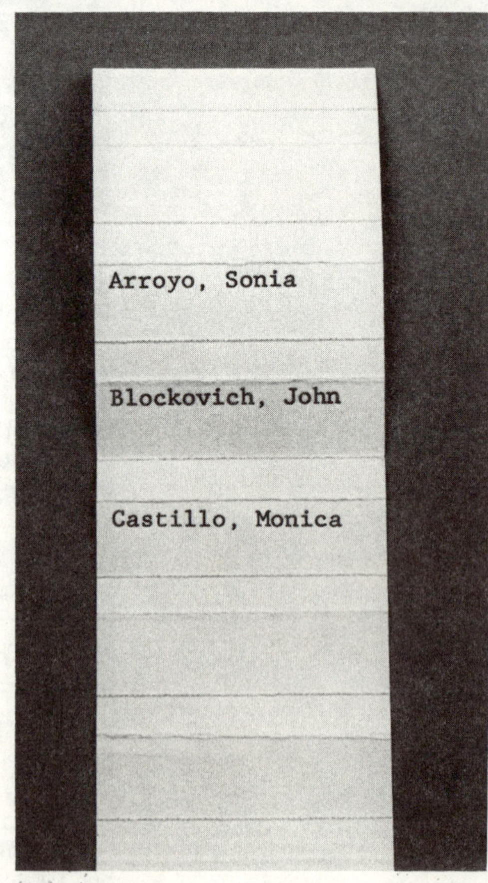

1. Using Form 3 for Job 2, type hanging folder labels for the 9 names given in Job 1. Follow the steps listed above. Remember to type on the line just below the crease.

2. Proofread and circle any errors you may have made.

JOB 3 EMPLOYEE AND CONVENTION BADGES

Form 4, page 119

READ ➤ People wear badges to identify themselves. Employees in large companies who need security clearance often must wear badges to enter their work areas. This kind of badge often has a photograph of the employee on it. Badges also are used at meetings such as conventions and conferences to identify the participants.

Name:	Jan Schneider
Emp. No.:	BII-D638
Dept.:	Drafting

Illustration 1
Employee badge

NATIONAL AUTOMATION CONFERENCE

LISA DAVIS

INTERTRON, INC.

Illustration 2
Convention badge

Follow these steps for typing badges:

Employee Badge	Convention Badge
1. Align the first guide word (*Name*) even with the top of the aligning scale, using the variable line spacer.	1. Begin 4 lines below the heading.
2. Set the left margin 2 spaces after the first guide word.	2. Set the left margin 5 spaces from the left edge of the badge.
3. Begin each line at this space.	3. Type the name in ALL CAPS. DS and type either the city and state or the company name (whichever is given) in ALL CAPS.

TYPE

1. Type the 8 badges for Job 3 using the information given below. Determine what information you need to include on each badge. Correct errors.

1. Type the information given in Illustration 1.

2. Type the information given in Illustration 2.

3. Mario Navjoks is from Minneapolis, MN.

4. M. J. Sipe works at 4D Corporation.

5. Shirley Skaggs is Employee No. 46 in the Production Department.

6. Daisuke Hayashi is Employee No. 130 in the Accounting Department.

7. Marsha Jacobsen is from Boston, MA.

8. James Tozer is Employee No. 98 in the Quality Control Department.

PROOFREAD/CHECK YES___ Continue ___NO Ask for help

2. Proofread and be sure that all errors are corrected. Is your typing done so well that you would be proud to wear each of the badges?

JOB 4 POSTAL CARDS

Form 5, page 117

Postal cards provide an easy means for the sender to give someone a brief amount of information. They are often used to find new customers. The customers show their interest in the company's offering by returning the postal reply card.

To prevent a postal card from slipping in your typewriter as you type, place the card in a "pocket" made from a folded sheet of paper. To make a pocket, follow these steps:

- Fold a sheet of paper (8½ x 11") in half (Fold 1).

- From the fold, fold the bottom half of the paper toward you ¼" or less to make a pocket (Fold 2). Tape the fold on both ends so it will not open.

- Place the postal card into the pocket right side up. Roll the paper and postal card into the typewriter.

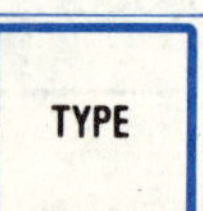

1. Separate the 4 cards on Form 5 along the perforations. Insert the first card in a pocket and roll it into the machine.

2. On one side, type the address as shown on the model (below). Take the card out and turn it over. Put it back in your typewriter and type the message on the back of the card, as shown on the model. Proofread and correct any errors you may have made.

3. Type the same address and message on the remaining 3 postal cards.

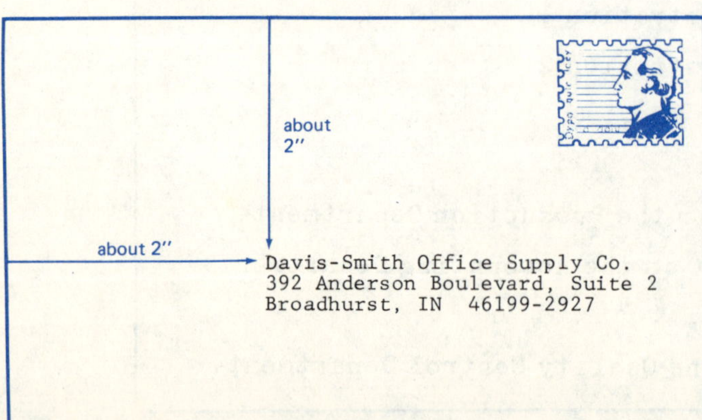

Save these cards to use in Unit 7, Job 3.

JOB 5 · ADDRESS CARDS *(5 × 3" Index Cards)*

Form 6, pages 113 and 115

For people or companies contacted frequently, address cards often are prepared and kept on file. Two kinds of cards used for this purpose are 5 × 3" index cards and smaller rotary file cards. Address cards may include brief biographical information. This serves as a useful reminder for sales representatives, insurance agents, or others when they talk with customers.

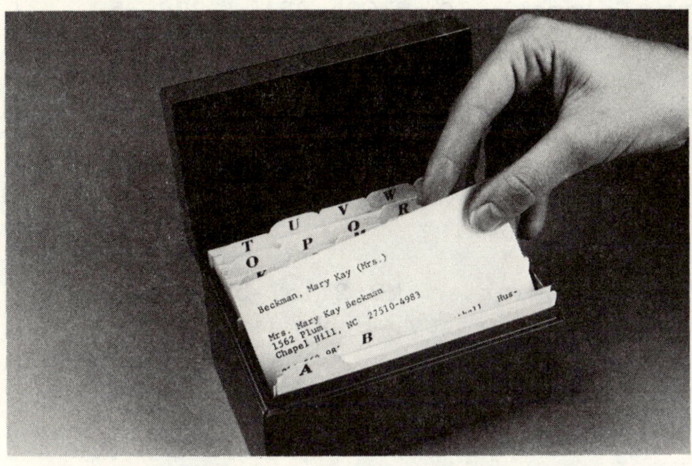

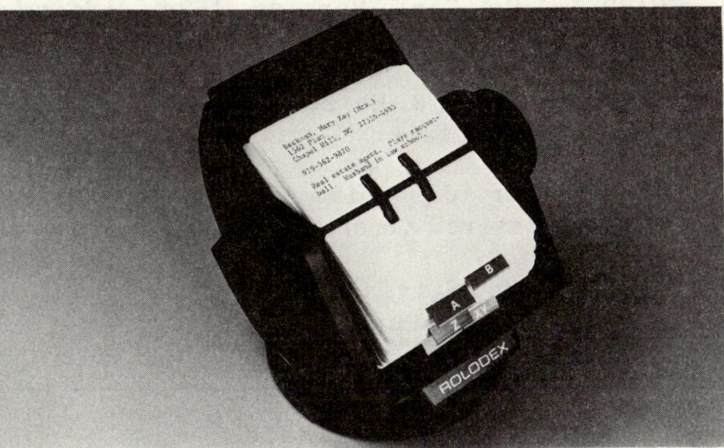

DO

In Job 5, you will type 5 × 3" index cards. Follow these instructions to type the 6 cards in this job.

1. Separate the 6 cards along the perforations. Insert a card, using a pocket to hold the card securely. Set your left margin 3 spaces from the left edge of the card. Begin to type on Line 3.

2. Decide the order under which the name to be typed will be filed. Most often, list people's names *last name first* and company names *first word first*.

TYPE

3. Type the first card, using the information given on the model address card (below). Follow the spacing guides given. Follow the same steps to type the other 5 address cards, using the information given on the *Mailing List* (page 48).

4. Proofread the cards when you finish and circle errors. Alphabetize the cards.

Line ⌐— 3 spaces from left edge of card

```
3 Beckman, Mary Kay (Mrs.)   ← list title last

TS

  Mrs. Mary Kay Beckman
  1562 Plum Street
  Chapel Hill, NC  27510-4983

DS

  919-562-9870

DS

  Real estate agent.  Plays racquetball.  Hus-
  band in law school.
```

MAILING LIST

JOBS 5 and 6

CARD 1:   Use the information given on the model.

CARD 2:   Mr. Michael L. Pitcher; 3610 South 1430 East; Boothbay Harbor, ME 00116-3496. 207-972-4454. Science teacher. Wife is an accountant. Hobby is fishing.

CARD 3:   Dr. Carla Morales; 1624 Griffin Lane; Caldwell, ID 83605-8211. 208-458-2252. M.D. specializing in family practice. Hobby is marathon running.

CARD 4:   Mr. A. B. Herseth; 400 East Lynwood; Detroit, MI 48231-6908. 313-553-4861. Automobile dealer. Is an avid semi-pro baseball player.

CARD 5:   Mr. Jose Diaz; 100 Armstrong Circle; Anaheim, CA 92807-7543. 714-991-5060. Retired aircraft worker. Hobbies are golf and bowling.

CARD 6:   Ms. Sylvia Wilmsen; 3500 Lynn Lee Park; Westminster, MD 21157-5208. 301-796-8273. Word processing supervisor. Husband owns pharmacy. Hobby is sailing.

JOB 6   ADDRESS CARDS *(Rotary File Cards)*

Form 7, page 113

Rotary file cards are smaller than index cards, so the format for typing an address on them is different. Notice on the model card (below) that you type the name and the address at the top.

1. Type 6 rotary file address cards, using a pocket (page 46) to hold each card securely. Use the same mailing list that you used for Job 5 (above). Spacing directions are given on the model card.

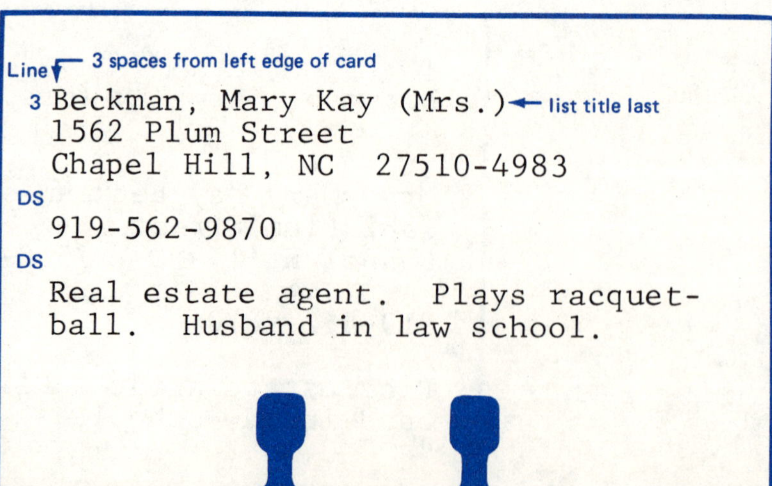

2. Proofread and circle any errors you may have made. Then, alphabetize the 6 cards.

Form 8, page 111

Job 7 is a CHALLENGE job which you will turn in to your teacher for approval when you finish. Try to complete the job in 20 minutes or less.

You are a member of the Skyview High School Boosters Club. Here is information about 3 people whom you have been asked to contact for contributions to the club.

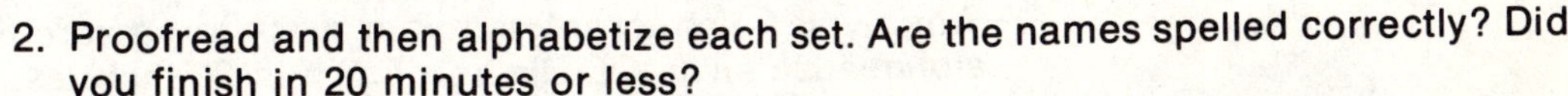

1. Sen. Geraldine Brown; 9552 Robin Way; Baton Rouge, LA 70811–9216. 572–8792. State senator. Advisor to S.H.S. Gymnastics Club.

2. Mr. Donald J. Cody; 800 Terra Linda Drive; Shreveport, LA 71110–3264. 1–279–4929. Plumber. Graduate of S.H.S. Avid S.H.S. football fan who attends every game.

3. Ms. Frances Franchino; 1004 Walden Place; Baton Rouge, LA 70806–5419. 579–0490. Manager of imported car dealership. Four children have graduated from S.H.S.

1. From the information given above, type the following for each person:

   a. Address card (5 × 3″ index card)

   b. Booster Club badge (Name in ALL CAPS; city in ALL CAPS)

   c. File folder label (refer to page 43 for guides if necessary)

   Correct any errors you make as you type.

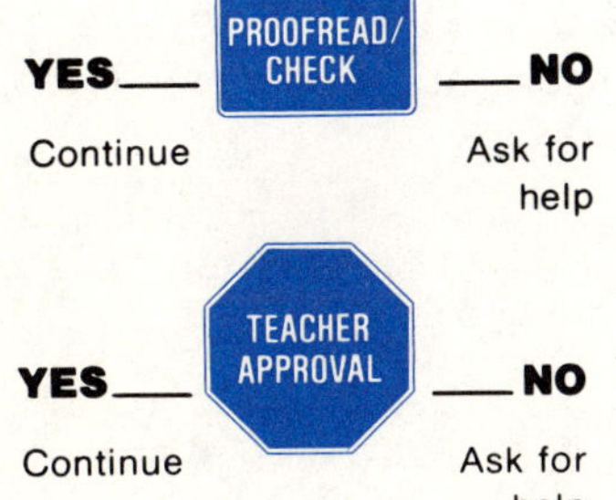

2. Proofread and then alphabetize each set. Are the names spelled correctly? Did you finish in 20 minutes or less?

3. Turn in Job 7 to your teacher for approval.

Form 9, page 109

As a member of the Membership Drive Committee of the Anderson Park Chamber of Commerce, you have been asked to contact 3 people and ask them to become members of the Chamber of Commerce.

1. Mr. Joseph Wagner; 132 Argonne Avenue; Anderson Park, CA 90300–6713. 421–7065. Owns Joe's Hobby and Crafts on Bellflower Boulevard. Hobbies are sailing and water skiing.

2. Ms. Pamela Jernigan; 1120 Ocean Boulevard; Anderson Park, CA 90300–6954. 432–2289. Manager of Anderson Park branch of 3rd Union Bank. Has pilot's license.

3. Ms. Linda Hernandez; 4182 Walton Street; Anderson Park, CA 90300–6962. 420–1957. Guidance counselor at Anderson Park High School. Former professional golfer.

Using the information given above, type the following for each person:

1. Address card

2. Chamber of Commerce badge (giving name and place of employment, all in CAPS)

3. File folder label

Correct any errors you may make as you work. Try to complete the job in 20 minutes or less.

When you finish, proofread your work to be sure that there are no errors. Then, alphabetize each set. Did you finish in 20 minutes or less?

YES___ **TEACHER APPROVAL** ___**NO**

Continue   Ask for
                  help

Turn in your test to your teacher.

6

VERTICALLY RULED FORMS

When you complete Unit 6, you will be able to type various business forms which are used in many offices.

Business forms are used . . . .

to request goods

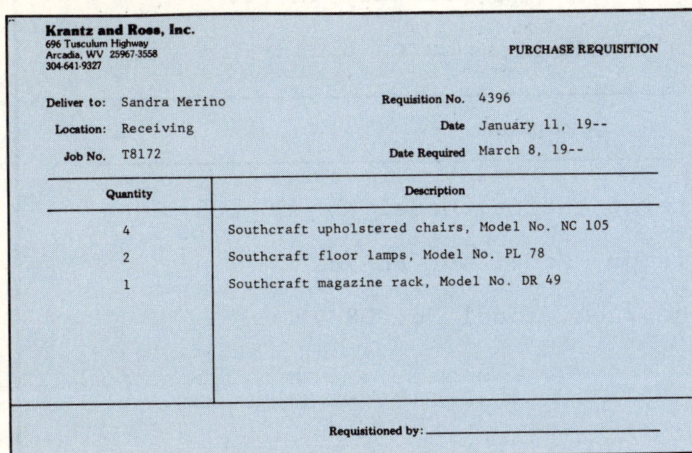

to order goods

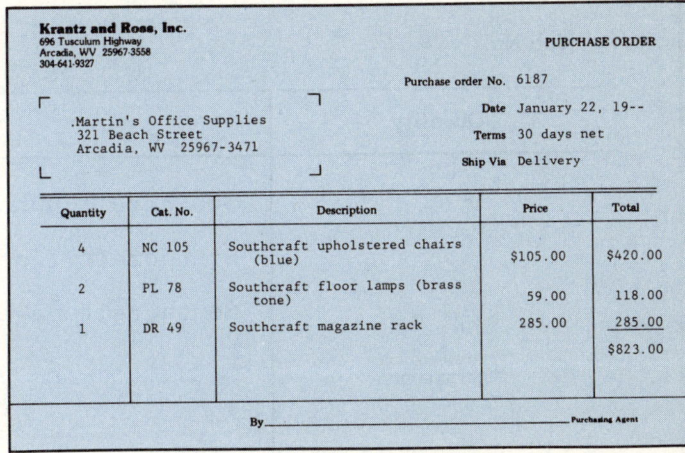

to sell goods

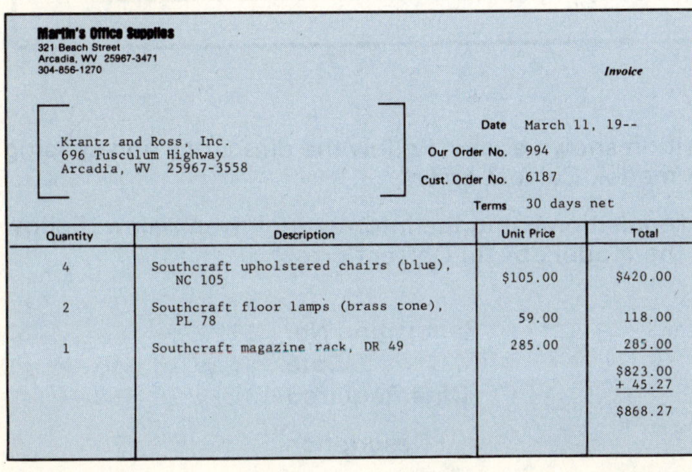

to pay for goods

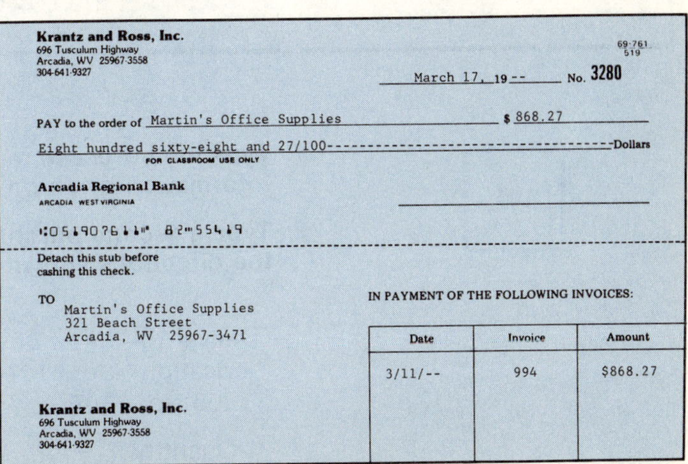

Forms are used in business to process data easily and quickly. Common to almost all businesses are forms used in the process of buying and selling goods. The way in which these forms are used depends on the size of the firms using them. In large firms, separate departments process the different forms, and computers may be used to calculate and print them. In small businesses, a purchasing agent or secretary may prepare and process all of the forms.

Form 10, page 107

The purchasing department is often responsible for buying goods, supplies, and equipment. By centralizing the buying in one department, quantity discounts can often be realized. When someone from another department wishes to purchase items, a *purchase requisition* must be completed and sent to the purchasing department.

Krantz and Ross, Inc.
696 Tusculum Highway
Arcadia, WV 25967-3558
304-641-9327

PURCHASE REQUISITION

Tab

Deliver to: Sandra Merino

Location: Receiving

Job No.   T8172

Requisition No.   4396

Date   January 11, 19--

Date Required   March 8, 19--

Quantity	Description
DS 4	Southcraft upholstered chairs, Model No. NC 105
2	Southcraft floor lamps, Model No. PL 78
1	Southcraft magazine rack, Model No. DR 49

Approximate Center

Tab 2 spaces from rule

Requisitioned by: ________________________________

1. Type the purchase requisition shown above. Follow the directions and spacing information given on the model. Correct errors.

2. Type a second purchase requisition using the information given below. Follow the directions shown on the model above. Correct errors.

Deliver to	Mark Dawson	Requisition No.	1772
Location	Supplies	Date	June 13, 19--
Job No.	305	Date Required	July 22, 19--

Quantity	Description
10 reams	Copier paper, 8½" × 11" (green), #P122G
1 dozen	Pencils, medium, #N512M
1 case	Rubber bands, 2" × 1/16", #A216S
1	Storage cabinet, 80" × 36" (gray), #E632G

3. Proofread the forms again correcting any errors you missed. Compare your copy *word for word* and *number for number* with the information for typing the forms. Did you follow the directions?

Form 11, page 105

When the purchasing department has received a purchase requisition, it may be necessary to get current prices or to compare prices between two suppliers to buy the goods at the lowest price. The purchasing department sends a *request for quotation* to suppliers. The request for quotation is *not* an order.

Krantz and Ross, Inc.
696 Tusculum Highway
Arcadia, WV 25967-3558
304-641-9327

Request for Quotation - - This is not an order.

To: *Martin's Office Supplies* ←SS heading
321 Beach Street
Arcadia, WV 25967-3471

Date Issued: *January 12, 19--*
Date Required: *March 8, 19--*

Quantity	Description
DS 4 2 1	*Southcraft upholstered chairs, Model No. NC 105* *Southcraft floor lamps, Model No. PL 78* *Southcraft magazine rack, Model No. DR 49*

↑
Approximate
Center

↑
Tab 2 spaces from rule
DS between items

1. Type the request for quotation shown above. Use the directions and spacing information given on the model. Correct errors.

2. Type a second request for quotation from the information given below. Follow the directions shown on the model above. Correct errors.

To: Martin's Office Supplies (see address on quotation request above)

Date issued: June 16, 19--   Date required: June 22, 19--

Requisitioned: paper, pencils, rubber bands, and storage cabinet as itemized on Purchase Requisition #2 (page 52). Include catalog numbers and description as given for the purchase requisition.

YES___ PROOFREAD/CHECK ___**NO**

Continue   Ask for
help

3. Proofread the forms again correcting any errors you missed. Compare your copy *word for word* and *number for number* with the information for typing the forms. Did you follow the directions?

Form 12, page 103

When goods or services are purchased, the buyer sends a purchase order to a supplier who sells the products listed on the purchase requisition. The purchase order must be carefully completed. Before typing a purchase order, check the arithmetic. Multiply the QUANTITY times UNIT PRICE to find the TOTAL. Then check the final total.

1. Type a purchase order from the model below. Use the directions and spacing information given on the model. Check the arithmetic to be sure the figures are correct. Correct errors as you type.

Krantz and Ross, Inc.
696 Tusculum Highway
Arcadia, WV 25967-3558
304-641-9327

Tab **PURCHASE ORDER**

Purchase order No.   6187

Martin's Office Supplies ← SS heading
321 Beach Street
Arcadia, WV   25967-3471

Date   January 22, 19--
Terms   30 days net
Ship Via   Delivery

Quantity	Cat. No.	Description	Price	Total
4	NC 105	Southcraft upholstered chairs (blue)	$ 105.00	$ 420.00
2	PL 78	Southcraft floor lamps (brass tone)	59.00	118.00
1	DR 49	Southcraft magazine rack	285.00	285.00
				$ 823.00

By _______________________ Purchasing Agent

---

2. Prepare to type a second purchase order for the **second** purchase requisition you typed in Job 1, page 52. Multiply the QUANTITY times the UNIT PRICE to find the TOTAL. Add the TOTAL column to find a final total.

Send the purchase order to Martin's Office Supplies.
Purchase order No.   03294
Date   June 30, 19--

Terms   30 days net
Ship Via   Delivery

Items are the same as those on Purchase Requisition #2 (page 52). Prices per unit are given below.

10 reams	P122G	copier paper, 8½" × 11" (green)	$ 2.29
1 dozen	N512M	pencils, medium	.65
1 case	A216S	rubber bands, 2" × 1/16"	5.74
1	E632G	storage cabinet, 80" × 36" × 18" (gray)	178.00

3. Proofread the forms. Correct errors you may have overlooked. Did you follow the spacing directions?

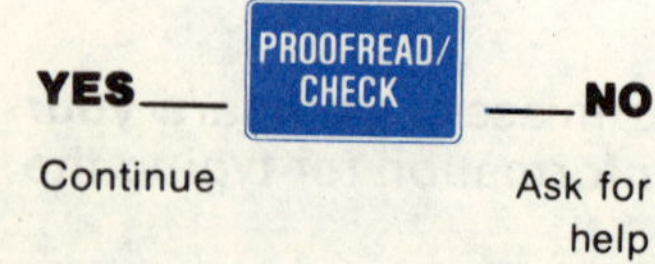

YES _____   _____ NO

Continue   Ask for
                  help

Form 13, page 101

When goods or services are sold, the seller prepares a bill, or an *invoice*. An invoice is prepared for each purchase order that is received. It bills the buyer for exactly the same items which are ordered on the purchase order. Before you type an invoice, always check to see that the figures are correct.

Martin's Office Supplies
321 Beach Street
Arcadia, WV 25967-3471
304-856-1270

Invoice

.Krantz and Ross, Inc.
696 Tusculum Highway
Arcadia, WV 25967-3558

Date   March 11, 19--
Our Order No.   994
Cust. Order No.   6187
Terms   30 days net

Quantity	Description	Unit Price	Total
4	Southcraft upholstered chairs (blue), NC 105	$ 105.00	$ 420.00
2	Southcraft floor lamps (brass tone), PL 78	59.00	118.00
1	Southcraft magazine rack, DR 49	285.00	$ 285.00 $ 823.00 + 45.27 $ 868.27

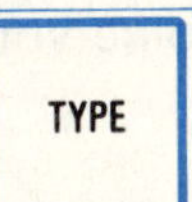

1. Type an invoice from the model above. Use the spacing information given on the model. Follow directions used to type previous forms. Correct errors.

2. Type a second invoice for the **second** purchase order you typed in Job 3, page 54. (Remember, an invoice is sent to the buyer, which is the company listed on the letterhead of the purchase order.) Other information you will need to complete this invoice follows:

Send the invoice to Krantz and Ross, Inc. (see address on invoice above).

> Date   July 15, 19--
> Our Order No.   1247
> Cust Order No.   03294
> Terms   30 days net

Find the total and then add sales tax of $12.13 to find the total amount invoiced. Look on page 77 of the *Answer Checkup* to see of your final total is correct.

3. Proofread the forms. Compare your typed copy *word for word* and *number for number* with the information for typing the forms. Check spacing. Correct any errors you overlooked.

YES___   **PROOFREAD/ CHECK**   ___**NO**
Continue   Ask for help

Form 14, page 99

When the buyer receives goods that have been ordered, the bill (invoice) is paid with a *voucher check*. A voucher check is a special check form with an attached stub that gives additional information about the check. The invoice number, any discounts which may be supplied, and the amount paid are shown on the stub. This gives the seller an explanation for the amount of payment.

Krantz and Ross, Inc.
696 Tusculum Highway
Arcadia, WV 25967-3558
304-641-9327

69-761
519

_______ March 17 19 -- _______   No. **3280**

PAY to the order of Martin's Office Supplies _______ $ 868.27 _______

Eight hundred sixty-eight and 27/100--- Dollars
FOR CLASSROOM USE ONLY

Arcadia Regional Bank
ARCADIA WEST VIRGINIA

⑈051907611⑈ 82⑈55419

- -

Detach this stub before
cashing this check.

TO

    Martin's Office Supplies
    321 Beach Street
    Arcadia, WV 25967-3471

IN PAYMENT OF THE FOLLOWING INVOICES:

Date	Invoice	Amount
3/11/--	994	$868.27

Krantz and Ross, Inc.
696 Tusculum Highway
Arcadia, WV 25967-3558
304-641-9327

1. Type a voucher check from the model above. Circle mistakes. Checks cannot be erased. In business if an error is made, the check must be retyped.

2. Type a second voucher check in payment of the second invoice you typed in Job 4, page 55. Information you will need is given below.

Make the check payable to Martin's Office Supplies. Date the check July 22, 19--. Spell out the amount as you did on the first voucher check (above). The information for the bottom half of the check is as follows:

date July 15, 19--
invoice 1247

YES____   ____ **NO**

Continue   Ask for
                   help

3. Proofread the forms and circle any mistakes you made.

Job 6 is a CHALLENGE job which you will turn in to your teacher for approval. Try to finish in 15 minutes.

Sometimes, after a purchase has been made, it is necessary for the seller to issue the buyer a *credit memorandum*. A credit memorandum credits the buyer's account. It is issued when the buyer returns goods or when goods are damaged on arrival. The credit memorandum shows the amount deducted from the buyer's account. Correct any errors you may make.

Martin's Office Supplies
321 Beach Street
Arcadia, WV 25967-3471
304-856-1270

CREDIT MEMORANDUM

Krantz and Ross, Inc.
696 Tusculum Highway
Arcadia, WV 25967-3558

Credit memorandum No. 433

Date April 12, 19--

Your order No. 6187

YOUR ACCOUNT HAS BEEN CREDITED FOR:

Quantity	Description	Cat. No.	Unit Price	Amount
2	Southcraft upholstered chairs (wrong color)	NC 105	$105.00	$210.00 + 11.55 $221.55

1. Type a credit memorandum from the above. Correct errors.

2. Type a second memorandum from the information below. Follow the same spacing that you followed on the model. Correct errors.

Send the credit memorandum to Krantz and Ross, Inc. Date the memo August 19, 19--. The memo number is 872. The memo is to be issued for 4 reams of copier paper, 8½ × 11" (green), order number is 03294, which was damaged upon receipt. Find the catalog number and the unit price on forms you typed previously for this order. To find the amount credited, multiply the *quantity* times the *unit price* and add $.50 sales tax. Look on page 77 of your *Answer Checkup* to see if your total amount is correct.

3. Proofread and correct any errors you may have overlooked. Turn the two forms in for approval.

Form 16, pages 93-95

In this unit, you have typed business forms in a sequence much like you would follow in a real job. For the test on this unit, you will type a *purchase requisition*, a *purchase order*, an *invoice*, and a *voucher check*, following the same order that you have followed in this unit. You will type the forms for one transaction from its requisition through its payment.

Type the 4 forms (pages 93-95) using the information given below. If you need help with the proper spacing for any of the forms, refer to the job in this unit which has a model form like the form you are typing. Correct any errors you may make as you work. Try to finish in 35 minutes.

Part 1:   Purchase Requisition
Job No. 26743
Deliver to Miriam Cintron
Location Customer Service Dept.
Req. No. 610
Date September 24, 19—
Date required November 12, 19—

   1   Omega terminal, OI–12
   2   Omega microcomputers w/2 disk drives, OI–44
   2   workstations, 48″ × 30″ × 26½″, walnut, OIS–2
200   8–inch floppy disks, double sided, double density, 236–8

Part 2:   Purchase Order
Send to: Datamart Stores
         Binney Plaza
         5881 Downs Highway
         Houston, TX   77901–5324
Order No. 26743
Date September 29, 19—
Terms 30 days net

Order the items requested on the purchase requisition (Part 1). Type a complete description of each item, as given for the purchase requisition. Unit prices are given below.

OI–12	Omega terminal	$ 750.00
OI–44	Omega microcomputer	4,298.00
OIS–2	workstation	344.00
236–8	8–inch floppy disk	3.65

Part 3:   Invoice
Send to: Gutierrez Industries
         46 Industrial Drive
         San Pedro, TX   78616–9216
Date November 12, 19—
Our Order No. P5273
Cust. Order No. 26743
Terms 30 days net

List the items shown in the purchase requisition (Part 1). Include the prices given for each in Part 2. Find the total amount and add sales tax of $430.56. Check on page 77 of the *Answer Checkup* to see if your total amount is correct.

Part 4:   Voucher Check
Make the check payable to Datamart Stores. Date the check November 23, 19—. Spell out the amount as you did on the other voucher checks in Unit 6. The information for the bottom half of the check is as follows:
date November 12, 19—
invoice P5273

Proofread the 4 forms carefully when you finish. Did you correct all errors? Are all the figures correct? Did you finish in 35 minutes?

Turn the test in to your teacher for approval.

YES____ TEACHER APPROVAL ____NO
Continue   Ask for
                help

PART 1 GOAL

To be able to adjust the typewriter for typing on horizontally ruled lines.

JOB 1 USING THE VARIABLE LINE SPACER AND ALIGNING SCALE

Half sheet/Form 17, page 91

DO

1. Space down to Line 10 on a half sheet of paper. Type and underline the words *aligning scale*.

   a. Notice the space which separates the letters from the underline. Take a special look at the relation of the letter *g* to the underline. Letters such as g, j, p, q, and y may touch the line on some machines.

   b. Now look at the relation between the underline and the top of the aligning scale. The underline should show just slightly below the aligning scale.

2. Space over 5 spaces from *aligning scale* and type another underline 20 spaces long. Take the form out of your typewriter.

3. Reinsert paper and align the typed line so it is in correct relation to the top of the aligning scale. Use the variable line spacer to roll the paper up or down as necessary. Type the words *papers agency injury*.

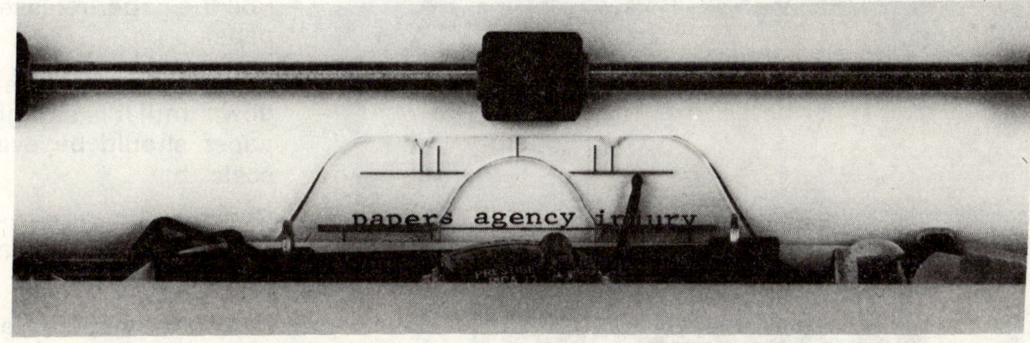

4. Compare your copy to the illustration above. Are the words *paper agency injury* positioned just slightly above the line? Do the letters *p, g, j,* and *y* almost or just touch the line? Repeat Steps 1, 2, and 3 if you need practice.

DO

5. Look at the two models on page 60. The first shows poor placement of the type on the printed form. The typist did not insert the form straight in the typewriter. This caused the type to go "downhill." The second model shows proper placement of type on the printed form.

NAME <u>Manuel Diaz-Flores</u>

REFERENCE NO. <u>ASD-44-390</u>

PHONE <u>641-2578</u>

AVAILABILITY DATE <u>September 17, 19--</u>

Check one: FULL-TIME <u> X </u>

                PART-TIME <u>   </u>   Model 1

NAME <u>Stacey Louchak</u>

REFERENCE NO. <u>CSD-51-084</u>

PHONE <u>763-9925</u>

AVAILABILITY DATE <u>April 6, 19--</u>

Check one: FULL-TIME <u> X </u>

                PART-TIME <u>   </u>   Model 2

TYPE

6. Using Form 17, p. 91, type the two forms using the information on the models above.

> **NOTE:** If the words start to touch the line, stop typing and straighten your paper. If your paper does not seem to be straight in the typewriter, try the method below to straighten paper.

- Pull the paper release lever (a) to loosen the paper.

- Straighten the paper by sliding it up or down until it is straight. The top edge of the paper should be even with the centering scale (b).

- Check to be sure that the left edge of the paper is perfectly straight against the paper guide (c).

- Return the paper release lever to its normal position.

- Use the variable line spacer (d) to align the horizontal lines with the aligning scale.

YES <u>   </u> PROOFREAD/CHECK <u>   </u> **NO**

Continue   Ask for help

7. Compare your finished forms with Model 2. Are your words aligned properly on the printed forms? If you need to practice typing on printed lines, an extra form is provided.

JOB 2 TYPING PARAGRAPHS ON RULED PAPER *(turn in for teacher approval)*

Form 18, page 91

1. Insert Form 18 and space down to the first ruled line. Align the paper so that the ruled line is slightly below the aligning scale. Check to be sure that the paper is inserted straight.

2. Set the margins for a 50-space line and set the line-space selector for DS. Set a tab stop 5 spaces from the left margin for your paragraph indentions.

3. Type the paragraphs given below. Listen for the bell to know when you are near the end of a line. When the bell rings, finish the word or divide it and finish typing it on the next line. Check on page 72 for guidelines on word division. Correct any errors you may make as you type.

In most office positions, you will need to know how to fill out various kinds of forms on the typewriter. Accuracy and neatness are necessary. Knowledge of the simple techniques *methods* used to position information onto forms is therefore very important.

To position words on forms, you must *be able* know how to adjust the typewriter to fit your typing on the lines. Exercises such as this one show *you* how to do this. You are learning skills now that can help you approach any form with confidence later on.

4. Proofread and correct any errors you may have missed. Are the words positioned correctly just above the lines? Turn in Job 2 for approval.

To be able to type on horizontally ruled forms.

JOB 3   POSTAL CARDS

Postal cards typed in Job 4, Unit 5 (page 46)

Fill in the 4 postal cards which you typed in Job 4, page 46, with the information given below. Use a pocket to hold each card in the typewriter.

1. Insert the card (in its pocket) to adjust it so that the ruled lines on the card are slightly below the aligning scale. Set the left margin near the beginning of the lines to be filled in.

Mrs. Julie Moe
Data Research, Inc.
129 East Third Avenue
Huntsville, AL 35816-5117
205-874-8764

Mr. Jay Garcia
P and N Printers
278 G Street
Merced, CA 95340-6197
209-542-8619

Mr. Ralph Schield
Dorf and Schield, Inc.
P. O. Box 1033
Janesville, WI 53547-2791
608-907-6538

Mrs. Sarah Kato
Kato and Kato, Inc.
2568 Aspen Boulevard
Aurora, CO 80045-3982
303-925-9841

2. Proofread and circle any errors you may have made. Compare each line with the information given above. Check the spelling of each name. Did you position the information slightly above the lines?

JOB 4   PERSONNEL REQUISITION FORM

Form 19, page 89

When a department needs to hire a new employee, the person who will supervise the new person fills out a *personnel requisition form* and gives it to the personnel department. From this information, the personnel department knows the kind of person to interview for the position.

1. Type a personnel requisition form. Use the information given on the form on page 63. Use the variable line spacer to align the horizontal lines correctly. Begin to type close to the beginning of each blank line.

2. Proofread and circle any errors. Did you type the form neatly and accurately?

Parin Products, Inc.

PERSONNEL REQUISITION

JOB TITLE _Receptionist_ DEPARTMENT _Marketing_

SALARY RANGE _$9,000 - 11,500_ REQUESTED BY _Anna Ling_

FULL-TIME _X_ PART-TIME _____ IF PART-TIME: DAILY HOURS ___________________

REGULAR _X_ TEMPORARY _____ IF TEMPORARY: LENGTH OF EMPLOYMENT ___________

DATE POSITION IS TO BE FILLED _March 11, 19--_ (earliest) _March 25, 19--_ (latest)

Specific job knowledge, experience, skills, licensing, educational background, etc. required (indicate by *) or desirable:

* High school diploma or equivalent
* Accurate typing at 45 wpm
* Machine dictation transcription (25 wpm for 10 minutes)
  Office education training (at postsecondary level)
  Good interpersonal skills

Specific duties and responsibilities for this position:

Greeting visitors
Answering multiline phone and screening telephone calls
Preparing correspondence (includes taking dictation)
Maintaining files
Handling routine mail

Department manager _M. J. Kowalski_ Date _February 26, 19--_

Approved by ___________________________ Date ___________

Use the information given on this model to type Form 19.

JOB 5   JOB APPLICATION FORM

Form 20, pages 85 and 87

When you apply for a job, you usually are asked to fill out a job application form. This form gives the interviewer the same facts about each applicant. The job application form can also reveal the applicant's skill at following directions, noticing details, and working neatly. A neat and complete job application form is an important step toward getting a job interview.

Sometimes you are asked to fill out the form at home. In this case, print or type the application, unless the directions ask for handwriting. Be thorough and careful as you work. Start at the beginning of the form and fill in each item exactly as requested. Be sure to list your name in the order specified. Whenever an item does not apply to you, write NA (for "not applicable") or draw a dash (—) in the blank. This shows the person reading your job application that you did see the item.

Parin Products, Inc.

APPLICATION FOR EMPLOYMENT

Parin Products does not discriminate in hiring or employment on the basis of race, color, religious creed, national origin, sex, or ancestry; or on the basis of age, against persons whose age is between 40 to 70, or on the basis of a handicap not limiting the applicant's ability to perform satisfactorily the job available. No question on this form is intended to secure information to be used for such discrimination. Parin Products will give this application every consideration. However, in accepting it, the company makes no commitment of employment to the applicant.

All questions must be completely and accurately answered.

GENERAL INFORMATION

NAME Malek (Last) Gilda (First) E. (Mid. Init.) DATE November 3, 1985

ADDRESS 2631 Poplar Drive PHONE 404-542-8937

Atlanta (City) GA (State) 30395-2611 (Zip) SS# 746-38-1558

WORK DESIRED: FULL-TIME X   PART-TIME ___ SEASONAL ___ PERMANENT X   TEMPORARY ___

Do you have any physical handicap which you feel would prevent you from performing certain kinds of work without significantly increasing the hazards to yourself, to others, or to the work facility? YES ___ NO X

If YES, describe: — —

Have you had any major illness in the past five (5) years which you feel would prevent you from performing certain kinds of work without significantly increasing the hazards to yourself, to others, or to the work facility? YES ___ NO X

If YES, describe: — —

Work time lost in the last two (2) years due to injury (# of days): — —

Have you ever been convicted of a felony? YES ___ NO X

If YES, describe: — —

Please indicate the type of work you desire and feel qualified to perform. Indicate your first choice by marking ONLY ONE (1) of the following: OFFICE/CLERICAL ___ MANUFACTURING ___ SHIPPING/WAREHOUSE ___

CUSTOMER SERVICE X   OTHER (list): ___

WORK EXPERIENCE   List present and past employment, beginning with the most recent (include part-time and seasonal).

COMPANY NAME Wheeler Auto Parts   Describe the work you did. Sales and

ADDRESS 1099 Prospect Place   customer service

Atlanta, GA 30328-7417

PHONE 404-846-3570   Employed (month/year) From 12/82 To present

SUPERVISOR Fred S. Wheeler   Reason for leaving: NA

COMPANY NAME Dee Dee's Deli   Describe the work you did. Sales

ADDRESS 50 Elm Street

Columbia, SC 29234-5254

PHONE 803-721-9546   Employed (month/year) From 7/81 To 12/82

SUPERVISOR D. S. DeRosa   Reason for leaving: Moved to Atlanta

COMPANY NAME The Clothes Closet   Describe the work you did. Cashier

ADDRESS 818 Parkway NW

Columbia, SC 29240-8133

PHONE 803-625-4719   Employed (month/year) From 6/80 To 6/81

SUPERVISOR Elaine Schmidt   Reason for leaving: Work/study program

REFERENCES   List three (do not list relatives).

NAME	ADDRESS	TELEPHONE NUMBER
Mr. Fred Wheeler	Please see address and phone number above.	
Ms. Jean Long	7528 Green Road, Atlanta, GA 30372-9518	404-771-1693
Dr. O. L. Jarvis	139 Florence, Columbia, SC 29218-8909	803-524-2865

May we ask your present employer about you? YES X   NOT UNTIL I GIVE NOTICE ___

I certify that the information given above is true to the best of my knowledge.

Signature *Gilda E. Malek*   Date November 3, 1985

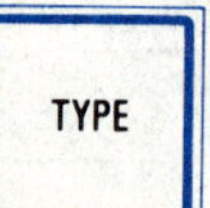

Fill out the 2-page job application form on your typewriter, using the information given on the next 2 pages.

1. Insert the first page of the form and align it so that the printed lines are slightly below the aligning scale.

2. Begin to type close to the beginning of each item. Set tab stops at points where you frequently begin to type. Backspace or space forward as necessary. Correct all errors neatly.

3. Proofread the page before you remove it from your machine. Remember, a job application form must be errorless.

4. Type the second page of the form, correcting all errors.

5. When you finish, check your work carefully. Did you complete each item? Are all errors corrected. Your form should look similar to the models shown above.

Parin Products, Inc.

APPLICATION FOR EMPLOYMENT

Parin Products does not discriminate in hiring or employment on the basis of race, color, religious creed, national origin, sex, or ancestry; or on the basis of age, against persons whose age is between 40 to 70, or on the basis of a handicap not limiting the applicant's ability to perform satisfactorily the job available. No question on this form is intended to secure information to be used for such discrimination. Parin Products will give this application every consideration. However, in accepting it, the company makes no commitment of employment to the applicant.

All questions must be completely and accurately answered.

GENERAL INFORMATION

NAME _Malek_ (Last) _Gilda_ (First) _E._ (Mid. Init.) DATE _November 3, 1985_

ADDRESS _2631 Poplar Drive_ PHONE _404-542-8937_

Atlanta (City) _GA_ (State) _30395-2611_ (Zip) SS# _746-38-1558_

WORK DESIRED: FULL-TIME _X_ PART-TIME ___ SEASONAL ___ PERMANENT _X_ TEMPORARY ___

Do you have any physical handicap which you feel would prevent you from performing certain kinds of work without significantly increasing the hazards to yourself, to others, or to the work facility? YES ___ NO _X_

If YES, describe: ______________________

Have you had any major illness in the past five (5) years which you feel would prevent you from performing certain kinds of work without significantly increasing the hazards to yourself, to others, or to the work facility? YES ___ NO _X_

If YES, describe: ______________________

Work time lost in the last two (2) years due to injury (# of days): ______________________

Have you ever been convicted of a felony? YES ___ NO _X_

If YES, describe: ______________________

Please indicate the type of work you desire and feel qualified to perform. Indicate your first choice by marking ONLY ONE (1) of the following: OFFICE/CLERICAL ______ MANUFACTURING ______ SHIPPING/WAREHOUSE ______

CUSTOMER SERVICE _X_ OTHER (list): ______________________

Job 5 (Job Application form, page 1)

WORK EXPERIENCE List present and past employment, beginning with the most recent (include part-time and seasonal).

COMPANY NAME _Wheeler Auto Parts_

ADDRESS _1099 Prospect Place_

Atlanta, GA 30328-7417

PHONE _404-846-3570_

SUPERVISOR _Fred S. Wheeler_

Describe the work you did. _Sales and customer service_

Employed (month/year) From _12/82_ To _present_

Reason for leaving: _NA_

COMPANY NAME _Dee Dee's Deli_

ADDRESS _50 Elm Street_

Columbia, SC 29234-5254

PHONE _803-721-9546_

SUPERVISOR _D. S. DeRosa_

Describe the work you did. _Sales_

Employed (month/year) From _7/81_ To _12/82_

Reason for leaving: _Moved to Atlanta_

COMPANY NAME _The Clothes Closet_

ADDRESS _818 Parkway NW_

Columbia, SC 29240-8133

PHONE _803-625-4719_

SUPERVISOR _Elaine Schmidt_

Describe the work you did. _Cashier_

Employed (month/year) From _6/80_ To _6/81_

Reason for leaving: _Work/study program_

REFERENCES List three (do not list relatives).

NAME	ADDRESS	TELEPHONE NUMBER
Mr. Fred Wheeler	Please see address and phone number above.	
Ms. Jean Long	7528 Green Road, Atlanta, GA 30372-9518	404-771-1693
Dr. O.L. Jarvis	139 Florence, Columbia, SC 29218-8909	803-524-2865

May we ask your present employer about you? YES _X_ NOT UNTIL I GIVE NOTICE ____

I certify that the information given above is true to the best of my knowledge.

Signature _(Student sign Gilda Malek's name.)_ Date _November 3, 1985_

JOB 6 CHALLENGE JOB *(turn in for teacher approval)*

Form 21, page 83

This job challenges you to fill out another kind of horizontally ruled form, a job recommendation form. Often, a company will ask those people listed as references by an applicant to fill out a recommendation form about the applicant.

TYPE

1. Type the form, using the information given on the model (below). Correct any errors you make as you work. Try to finish the form in 15 minutes or less.

PARIN PRODUCTS, INC.

REQUEST FOR RECOMMENDATION

The person named below has applied for a job with Parin Products and has listed you as a reference. Please complete this recommendation form at your earliest convenience and use our envelope to return it to us. We appreciate your assistance.

NAME OF APPLICANT *Miriam C. Ackley*

APPLICANT'S ADDRESS *1906 Jefferson Boulevard*
Atlanta, GA 30303-6724

POSITION APPLIED FOR *General mechanic*

GENERAL DUTIES *General maintenance and repair of trucks and autos in our service fleet.*

1. How long have you known applicant? *2½ years* In what capacity have you known applicant? *She worked as a general mechanic for Wheeler Flight Service, Macon, Georgia.*

2. Has applicant had previous experience of the nature described in the position applied for above while under your supervision? Yes *X* No____

   How long? *1½ years* Duties *Miriam had responsibility for routine maintenance on our propeller aircraft.*

3. Is applicant honest? Yes *X* No____   Is applicant dependable? Yes *x* No____

   Comments *Miriam also had responsibility for purchasing replacement parts. She kept excellent records.*

4. Does applicant work well with others? Yes *X* No____

   Comments *Miriam has excellent mechanical skills and is very personable.*

5. List any strengths or weaknesses as you see them *Miriam has no real weaknesses; however, she is improving her electrical skills.*

6. Please add any additional comments you may wish to make *Miriam did an excellent job and rarely missed work. Personal reasons compelled her to move to Atlanta.*

________________________________   ________________
(Signature)   (Date)

---

2. Proofread carefully. Be sure all errors are neatly corrected.

3. After you have checked your typing, take the form out of your machine and sign and date the recommendation form. Did you finish in 15 minutes or less?

4. Turn in Job 6 to your teacher for approval.

PROOFREAD/CHECK

YES____   ____NO

Continue   Ask for help

REVIEW: KEY CONCEPTS FOR UNIT 7

From this list of terms, fill in the blanks below. *Use each term once only.*

> *variable line spacer*
> *tab stop*
> *paper release lever*
> *aligning scale*

1. For good placement on most typewriters, the lines on which you are typing should appear slightly below the ________________ ________________.

2. To change the line spacing permanently, use the ________________ ________________ ________________.

3. If your paper is in your typewriter crooked, use the ________________ ________________ ________________.

4. Set a ________________ ________________ for paragraph indentions.

Fill in the blanks below.

1. Indent ________ spaces for a paragraph unless directions are otherwise.

2. Give the *left* and *right* margins for a 50-space line on a pica typewriter. Use the space below to figure your answers.

   PICA: Left margin = ________   Right margin = ________

3. Give the *left* and *right* margins for a 50-space line on an elite typewriter. Use the space below to figure your answers.

   ELITE: Left margin = ________   Right margin = ________

4. When increased workload indicates that an additional employee should be hired, the department manager submits a ________________________________. ________________ form to the personnel department describing the needed employee's qualifications.

5. The personnel department advertises the company's need for a new employee and applicants for the position fill out a ________________________________. ________________ form.

Check on page 77 of your Answer Checkup to see if you have answered these questions correctly. If you do not understand an answer, ask your teacher for help.

Form 22, page 81

Most employees are asked periodically to analyze their jobs and their progress on the job. Using Form 22 on page 81, type a self-appraisal form with the information given in the model (below). Apply the skills you have learned for typing horizontally ruled forms. Neatly correct any errors you make. Try to finish in 12 minutes or less.

Parin Products, Inc.

EMPLOYEE SELF-APPRAISAL

NAME *Michael Ackley*

POSITION TITLE *Receptionist, Marketing Department*

DUTIES: List the job duties which you perform most frequently in your position:

Greeting visitors, answering phone, preparing corre-spondence, handling mail, maintaining files.

WORK TRAITS: Using the RATINGS scale given, rate your work traits on these items:

> **RATINGS**
>
> **5** Performance significantly exceeds the standard required for this position.
>
> **4** Performance is consistently above the standard required for this position.
>
> **3** Performance meets the standard required for this position.
>
> **2** Performance is consistently below the standard required for this position.
>
> **1** Performance is significantly below the standard required for this position.
>
> **NA** Not Applicable.

3 ATTITUDE/ADJUSTMENT TO WORK ENVIRONMENT: I respond positively to instructions and suggestions. I demonstrate flexibility in adapting to changes in procedures, technology, etc. I work independently and do not disturb others.

3 COMMUNICATION/INTERPERSONAL RELATIONSHIPS: I am effective in oral and written communications. I listen well. I work well with others and am sensitive to their needs and viewpoints.

4 TIME MANAGEMENT/VOLUME OF WORK: I demonstrate effective use of time and establish priorities when necessary. I produce the expected volume of work.

3 QUALITY/DEPENDABILITY: I produce work which is accurate, thorough, and neat. I follow instructions and meet deadlines with a minimum of supervision. I am punctual and have a good attendance record.

EVALUATION: Fill in the blanks below:

1. Do you feel that your job performance contributes to your department's overall effectiveness? YES **X** NO ___

    Explain: *I am able to help many callers without consulting the marketers.*

2. What part(s) of your job do you enjoy the most? *Interacting with the visitors, callers, and employees in the department.*

    What do you enjoy the least? *Checking supplies in stock.*

3. What can you do (or what are you currently doing) to improve your skills? *I have been taking an evening class in data processing.*

When you finish typing, proofread to make sure that you have corrected all errors. Did you finish in 12 minutes?

Turn in your test to your teacher.

APPENDIX

1. Divide words <u>only</u> between syllables. (A one-syllable word, such as <u>work</u>, would not be divided.)

   car-pet   bun-dle   cal-en-dar   to-mor-row

2. Do not divide words of five or fewer letters, even though they may have more than one syllable.

   other   tiny   idea   even

3. There must be <u>more</u> than one letter with the first part of the word and <u>more</u> than two letters with the last part of the word.

   in-sult (<u>but not i-deals</u>)   king-dom (<u>but not speak-er</u>)

4. Hyphenated compound words should only be divided at the hyphen.

   good-looking   old-fashioned   self-centered

5. Avoid dividing a contraction (<u>isn't</u>) or a single group of figures.

   haven't (<u>not have-n't</u>) $1,234

6. When it is necessary to divide a date, a proper name, or an address, divide at the logical point for readability.

May 13,—1984 (<u>not May—13, 1984</u>)
Mr. Jack—Brown (<u>not Mr.—Jack Brown</u>)
Cincinnati,—OH 45227 (not Cincinnati, OH—45227)

7. Usually divide a word between double consonants:

   sum-mer   kit-ten   fid-dle   win-ner

   If, however, a suffix (ie., -ing, ed) is added to a root word that ends in double letters, divide after the double letters of the root word.

8. When the final consonant is doubled in adding a suffix (ie., -ing, -en,), divide between the double letters.

   run-ning   let-ting   begin-ning

9. Divide after a one-letter syllable within a word; however, when two single-letter syllables occur together, divide between them.

   sepa-rate   regu-late   gradu-ation

10. When the one-letter syllable <u>a</u>, <u>i</u>, or <u>u</u>, is followed by the ending ly, ble, cle, or cal, divide before the one-letter syllable.

    stead-ily   siz-able   cler-ical (<u>but practi-cal</u>)

Using the rules listed above, divide the following words. Check Answer Key, page 77.

1. **possess** _______________________________
2. **willing** _______________________________
3. **popular** _______________________________
4. **motivation** ____________________________
5. **hammer** ________________________________
6. **strong-minded** _________________________
7. **niece** __________________________________
8. **seedling** _______________________________
9. **shouldn't** ______________________________
10. **good-natured** __________________________
11. **August 24, 1944** _______________________
12. **running** _______________________________
13. **knitting** _______________________________
14. **compatible** ____________________________
15. **symphony** _____________________________
16. **employment** ___________________________
17. **situation** ______________________________
18. **$5,419** _________________________________

The bell on the typewriter acts as a warning that the margin is near. Depending on the machine, the bell rings 6 to 11 spaces before the margin locks. If your typewriter bell rang 11 spaces before the desired margin, it would be difficult to keep track of these spaces. Therefore, most typists set their right margin so that the bell will ring 5 spaces before the desired margin. These 5 spaces allow enough time for the typist to either finish a word or divide it. To learn to set your margin stop so that the bell will ring 5 spaces before the desired margin setting, complete the following drill:

Drill 1

1. Set margin stops for an exact 60-space line (pica, 12 and 72; elite, 21-81).

2. Type as much of the following sentence as you can before the bell rings. Stop as soon as the bell rings.

   Move stop so bell rings 5 spaces before desired line ending.

3. Instead of typing the rest of the sentence, type consecutive numbers (1234 etc.) until the margin locks. The last number typed is the number of spaces between the bell and the space where the margin locks (11 in example below).

   Move stop so bell rings 5 spaces before desired li12345678901

4. Subtract 5 spaces from the number of figures typed in Step 3.

   11 digits typed − 5 spaces = 6 spaces

5. Move the right margin set one space to the right for each space in the difference you found in Step 4.

   Pica: 72 + 6 spaces = 78 margin setting
   Elite: 81 + 6 spaces = 87 margin setting

6. Type the sentence again. Your bell should ring at the following space: pica, 67; elite, 76.

   Move stop so bell rings 5 spaces before desired line end ◄ BELL RINGS

Drill 2

Using the same margin setting you found in Drill 1, type the paragraph below. Listen for the bell to determine line endings. Divide words as needed. When the bell rings, you know you will have 5 spaces to either finish or divide the word you are typing. Your line endings should be just like those shown below.

```
    Typewriters vary widely in terms of the number of char-

acters they will permit to be typed between the point where

the warning bell rings and the point at which the carriage

or carrier locks.
```

DESIRED MARGIN SETTINGS

Shown at the right are the margins for 1″, 1½″, and 2″ side margins. So that your bell will ring 5 spaces before the right margin, add the figure you determined in Step 4, Drill 1, to the settings listed for the right margins (75, pica; 90, elite).

Drill 3

Retype the paragraph in Drill 2 using 1″ side margins rather than a 60-space line. Make bell adjustment. Check the *Answer Checkup*, p. 76, to see if your line endings are correct.

	Pica	Elite
1″ margins	10—75	12—90
1½″ margins	15—70	18—84
2″ margins	20—65	24—78

Errors are usually corrected by one of the following:

Eraser

When erasing, use a light touch. Do not allow eraser crumbs to drop into the typewriter. Be careful not to tear the paper. Follow these steps:

1. Lift the paper bail and turn the paper toward you if the error is on the upper two thirds of the page or away from you if the error is on the lower third of the page.

2. Move the carriage or element to the extreme right or left so that it is easy to get at the error.

3. Use an eraser shield to protect typing that is not to be erased.

4. Erase the error. Brush or blow the eraser crumbs from the paper.

5. Make the correction.

Correction Fluid

Correction fluid covers or masks the error with a liquid which leaves a white enamel-like material on the paper. Follow these steps when using correction fluid:

1. Turn the paper up a few spaces.

2. Shake the correction fluid bottle; remove the applicator brush and daub excess liquid on inside of bottle opening.

3. Apply liquid sparingly to error. Be sure to cover the entire error.

4. Blow on error to speed up drying process.

5. When liquid is dry, type the correction.

Correction Paper

Correction paper covers the error with a powder-like substance. There are several types, such as correction tape and correction paper strips. Follow these steps when using correction paper:

1. Backspace to the beginning of error.

2. Place the correction tape or paper strip behind the typewriter ribbon and in front of the error, coated side toward the paper.

3. Retype the error exactly as you made it. In this step, powder from the correction paper is pressed by force of the keystroke into the form of the error, thus masking it.

4. Remove the correction paper. Backspace to the point at which the correction is to be made and then type the correction.

Lift-off Tape/Ribbon

Typewriters equipped with a lift-off tape or ribbon system offer the fastest and easiest method of correcting errors. Follow these steps when using a lift-off tape or ribbon system:

1. When an error is made, move back to the error and strike the correction key on the typewriter.

2. Strike the incorrect character again and the error will be lifted off or covered over.

3. Type the correct character.

PROOFREADER'S MARKS

Mark	Meaning	Example
ℰ	Take out; delete	Delete these ~~very unnecessary~~ words.
∧	Insert copy shown	Insert copy shon.
#	Insert a space	Insert a space whenneeded.
Cap (or) ≡	Capitalize	the first word of a sentence begins with a capital letter.
lc (or) /	Lowercase	Do not capitalize Incorrectly.
∧	Insert comma	Do not omit this comma and the sentence will be correct.
___	Underline or italics	Underline the title of a book, such as *The Sound and the Fury*.
SS	Single-space	3. When typing entries for enumerated items, single-space the second line of each entry.
DS	Double-space	DOUBLE-SPACE AFTER A MAIN HEADING
TS	Triple-space	Triple-space After a Secondary Heading
⊐	Move to the left	Move copy to the left.
⊏	Move to the right	Move copy to the right.
∼	Transpose; turn around	To transpose is to around turn copy.
⊙	Insert period	Insert a period at the end of a sentence.
⌒	Close up space	Close up a spac e when needed.
stet	Let it stand	Let ~~these words stand~~.
No ¶	No paragraph	Do not begin a paragraph here.
⊙ sp	Spell out	1 rule is to spell out a figure beginning a sentence.
⊓	Move up	Move this copy up.
⊔	Move down	Move this copy down.

ANSWER CHECKUP

UNIT 1

page 5 (Job 4)

0 + 55 = 55 ÷ 2 = 27 (pica); 0 + 66 = 66 ÷ 2 = 33 (elite)

page 7 (Review: Key Concepts for Unit 1)

1. across
2. 0
3. add, 2
4. 10
5. 12
6. Find out which you are using.
7. center
8. center
9. 1
10. 42
11. 51
12. 2
13. 1
14. 5½" × 10 characters/inch = 55 pica characters
    55 ÷ 2 = 27
15. 3" × 12 characters/inch = 36 elite characters
    36 ÷ 2 = 18

UNIT 2

page 12 (Job 3)

$33 - 14 = 19 \div 2 = 9 + 1 = $ Line 10.

page 13 (Job 4)

$66 - 37 = 29 \div 2 = 14 + 1 = $ Line 15.

page 15 (Job 5)

2. $51 - 23 = 28 \div 2 = 14 + 1 = $ Line 15.

3. Pica: 5½" × 10 characters/inch = 55 pica characters
   Center—55 ÷ 2 = 27   Left margin—27 − 20 = 7   Right margin—27 + 20 = 47 + 5 = 52

   Elite: 5½" × 12 characters/inch = 66 elite characters
   Center—66 ÷ 2 = 33   Left margin—33 − 20 = 13   Right margin—33 + 20 = 53 + 5 = 58

page 17 (Review: Key Concepts for Unit 2)

1. 1
2. 2
3. triple
4. double
5. triple
6. main
7. up and down

8. 1) Find the number of lines available on the paper.
   2) Count the lines needed to type the job.
   3) Subtract the number of lines needed to type the job from the lines available on the paper.
   4) Divide by 2 (drop any remaining fraction).
   5) Add 1 line and begin to type on that line.

9. 6
10. 7
11. 33
12. 51

13. $33 - 11 = 22 \div 2 = 11 + 1 = $ Line 12.
14. $51 - 33 = 18 \div 2 =\ \ 9 + 1 = $ Line 10.

UNIT 3

page 22 (Job 4)

Pica: left margin—29   tab stop—47

Elite: left margin—38   tab stop—56

page 23 (Job 5)

Pica: left margin—16   tab stops—34, 52

Elite: left margin—25   tab stops—43, 61

page 27 (Review: Key Concepts for Unit 3)

1. 6
2. $66 - 37 = 29 \div 2 = 14 + 1 = $ 15. Begin typing on Line 15.
3. $33 - 15 = 18 \div 2 = 9 + 1 = $ 10. Begin typing on Line 10.
4. longest
5. columns
6. left
7. 1, 1
8. right
9. B

UNIT 4

(page 29)

Column A—heading centered over column   Column B—column centered under heading

page 30 (Job 1)

Pica: Drill 1—33, 47
      Drill 2—30, 51
Elite: Drill 1—42, 56
      Drill 2—39, 60

page 31 (Job 2)

	Pica	Elite
Left margin	23	32
Tab stop	51	60
Col. 1 heading	28	37
Col. 2 heading	53	62

page 37 (Job 7)

Animal Name + Stallion + Female + Young + 18 spaces

page 38 (Job 8)

	Pica	Elite
Left margin	14	23
Col. 2 tab stop	37	46
Col. 3 tab stop	64	73

page 39 (Job 9) (Remember to set tabs at the points which require the least spacing forward or backspacing.)

	Pica	Elite
Left margin	9	18
Begin Col. 2	37	46
Begin Col. 3	49	58
Begin Col. 4	65	74

page 41 (Review: Key Concepts for Unit 4)

1. longer
2. shorter
3. triple
4. double
5. longer
6. 1, 2
7. 1, 2
8. 15
9. 18
10. single
11. double
12. 1
13. at the "ones" column of the whole numbers
14. longest
15. at the decimal point

UNIT 6

page 55 (Job 4)

Total for second invoice is $219.42.

page 57 (Job 6)

Total for second credit memo is $9.66.

page 58 (Test)

Total amount is $11,194.56

UNIT 7

page 68 (Review: Key Concepts for Unit 7)

1. aligning scale
2. variable line spacer
3. paper release lever
4. tab stop

1. 5
2. Left margin—17   Right margin—67 + 5 = 72
3. Left margin—26   Right margin—76 + 5 = 81
4. personnel requisition
5. job application

APPENDIX

page 72 (Word-Division Drill)

1. pos-sess
2. will-ing
3. popu-lar
4. mo-ti-va-tion
5. ham-mer
6. strong-minded
7. niece
8. seed-ling
9. shouldn't
10. good-natured
11. August 24,-1944
12. run-ning
13. knit-ting
14. com-pat-ible
15. sym-phony
16. em-ploy-ment
17. situ-ation
18. $5,419

page 73 (Drill 3, Pica solution)

```
    Typewriters vary widely in terms of the number of characters

they will permit to be typed between the point where the warning

bell rings and the point at which the margin locks.
```

(Elite solution)

```
    Typewriters vary widely in terms of the number of characters they will

permit to be typed between the point where the warning bell rings and the point

at which the margin locks.
```

STUDENT CHECK SHEET

Directions: Keep track of your progress by recording the date you complete each job. Then rate your typing with a +, √, or − according to the criteria below. Record your test scores as well.

+ No format errors and good typing accuracy
√ One major or two minor errors in format and average typing accuracy
− Two or more format errors and many typing errors

UNIT 1   HORIZONTAL CENTERING

Job No.	Date Completed	Self-Rating
1		
2		
3		
4		
5		
6		
Key Concepts		
Test Grade		

UNIT 2   VERTICAL CENTERING

Job No.	Date Completed	Self-Rating
1		
2		
3		
4		
5		
6		
Key Concepts		
Test Grade		

UNIT 3   TABLE TYPING, NO COLUMN HEADINGS

Job No.	Date Completed	Self-Rating
1		
2		
3		
4		
5		
6		
7		
8		
9		
Key Concepts		
Test Grade		

Job No.	Date Completed	Self-Rating
1		
2		
3		
4		
5		
6		
7		
8		
9		
10		
Key Concepts		
Test	Grade	

UNIT 5   UNRULED FORMS

Job No.	Date Completed	Self-Rating
1		
2		
3		
4		
5		
6		
7		
Test	Grade	

UNIT 6   VERTICALLY RULED FORMS

Job No.	Date Completed	Self-Rating
1		
2		
3		
4		
5		
6		
Test	Grade	

UNIT 7   HORIZONTALLLY RULED FORMS

Job No.	Date Completed	Self-Rating
1		
2		
3		
4		
5		
6		
Key Concepts		
Test	Grade	

Parin Products, Inc.

EMPLOYEE SELF-APPRAISAL

NAME ____

POSITION TITLE ____

DUTIES: List the job duties which you perform most frequently in your position:

____

____

____

WORK TRAITS: Using the RATINGS scale given, rate your work traits on these items:

> **RATINGS**
>
> **5** Performance significantly exceeds the standard required for this position.
>
> **4** Performance is consistently above the standard required for this position.
>
> **3** Performance meets the standard required for this position.
>
> **2** Performance is consistently below the standard required for this position.
>
> **1** Performance is significantly below the standard required for this position.
>
> **NA** Not Applicable.

______ ATTITUDE/ADJUSTMENT TO WORK ENVIRONMENT: I respond positively to instructions and suggestions. I demonstrate flexibility in adapting to changes in procedures, technology, etc. I work independently and do not disturb others.

______ COMMUNICATION/INTERPERSONAL RELATIONSHIPS: I am effective in oral and written communications. I listen well. I work well with others and am sensitive to their needs and viewpoints.

______ TIME MANAGEMENT/VOLUME OF WORK: I demonstrate effective use of time and establish priorities when necessary. I produce the expected volume of work.

______ QUALITY/DEPENDABILITY: I produce work which is accurate, thorough, and neat. I follow instructions and meet deadlines with a minimum of supervision. I am punctual and have a good attendance record.

EVALUATION: Fill in the blanks below:

1. Do you feel that your job performance contributes to your department's overall effectiveness? YES _____   NO _____

   Explain: ____

   ____

2. What part(s) of your job do you enjoy the most? ______________________

   ____

   What do you enjoy the least? ____

3. What can you do (or what are you currently doing) to improve your skills? ___________

   ____

PARIN PRODUCTS, INC.

REQUEST FOR RECOMMENDATION

The person named below has applied for a job with Parin Products and has listed you as a reference. Please complete this recommendation form at your earliest convenience and use our envelope to return it to us. We appreciate your assistance.

NAME OF APPLICANT____

APPLICANT'S ADDRESS____

____

POSITION APPLIED FOR____

GENERAL DUTIES____

____

1. How long have you known applicant?__________________ In what capacity have you known

   applicant?____

   ____

2. Has applicant had previous experience of the nature described in the position applied for above

   while under your supervision?   Yes____No____

   How long?________________ Duties____

   ____

3. Is applicant honest?   Yes____ No____   Is applicant dependable?   Yes____ No____

   Comments____

   ____

4. Does applicant work well with others?   Yes____ No____

   Comments____

   ____

5. List any strengths or weaknesses as you see them___________________________________

   ____

6. Please add any additional comments you may wish to make_____________________________

   ____

   ____

____   ___________________________
            (Signature)   (Date)

Parin Products, Inc.

APPLICATION FOR EMPLOYMENT

Parin Products does not discriminate in hiring or employment on the basis of race, color, religious creed, national origin, sex, or ancestry; or on the basis of age, against persons whose age is between 40 to 70, or on the basis of a handicap not limiting the applicant's ability to perform satisfactorily the job available. No question on this form is intended to secure information to be used for such discrimination. Parin Products will give this application every consideration. However, in accepting it, the company makes no commitment of employment to the applicant.

All questions must be completely and accurately answered.

GENERAL INFORMATION

NAME ____ DATE _________________________________
     (Last)   (First)   (Mid. Init.)

ADDRESS ____ PHONE _________________________________

____ SS# _________________________________
     (City)   (State)   (Zip)

WORK DESIRED: FULL-TIME ____ PART-TIME ____ SEASONAL ____ PERMANENT ____ TEMPORARY ____

Do you have any physical handicap which you feel would prevent you from performing certain kinds of work without significantly increasing the hazards to yourself, to others, or to the work facility?   YES ____   NO ____

If YES, describe: ____

Have you had any major illness in the past five (5) years which you feel would prevent you from performing certain kinds of work without significantly increasing the hazards to yourself, to others, or to the work facility?   YES ____   NO ____

If YES, describe: ____

Work time lost in the last two (2) years due to injury (# of days): ____

Have you ever been convicted of a felony?   YES ____   NO ____

If YES, describe: ____

Please indicate the type of work you desire and feel qualified to perform. Indicate your first choice by marking ONLY ONE (1) of the following: OFFICE/CLERICAL ______   MANUFACTURING ______   SHIPPING/WAREHOUSE ______

CUSTOMER SERVICE ______   OTHER (list): ____

WORK EXPERIENCE   List present and past employment, beginning with the most recent (include part-time and seasonal).

COMPANY NAME _______________________   Describe the work you did. _______________________

ADDRESS _______________________   _______________________

_______________________   Employed (month/year)
From _______________________   To _______________

PHONE _______________________

SUPERVISOR _______________________   Reason for leaving: _______________________

COMPANY NAME _______________________   Describe the work you did. _______________________

ADDRESS _______________________   _______________________

_______________________   Employed (month/year)
From _______________________   To _______________

PHONE _______________________

SUPERVISOR _______________________   Reason for leaving: _______________________

COMPANY NAME _______________________   Describe the work you did. _______________________

ADDRESS _______________________   _______________________

_______________________   Employed (month/year)
From _______________________   To _______________

PHONE _______________________

SUPERVISOR _______________________   Reason for leaving: _______________________

REFERENCES   List three (do not list relatives).

NAME	ADDRESS	TELEPHONE NUMBER

May we ask your present employer about you?   YES _____   NOT UNTIL I GIVE NOTICE _____

I certify that the information given above
is true to the best of my knowledge.

Signature _______________________   Date _______________________

Parin Products, Inc.

APPLICATION FOR EMPLOYMENT

Parin Products does not discriminate in hiring or employment on the basis of race, color, religious creed, national origin, sex, or ancestry; or on the basis of age, against persons whose age is between 40 to 70, or on the basis of a handicap not limiting the applicant's ability to perform satisfactorily the job available. No question on this form is intended to secure information to be used for such discrimination. Parin Products will give this application every consideration. However, in accepting it, the company makes no commitment of employment to the applicant.

All questions must be completely and accurately answered.

GENERAL INFORMATION

NAME ____ DATE _____________________________
     (Last)   (First)   (Mid. Init.)

ADDRESS ____ PHONE ____________________________

____ SS# ___________________________________
     (City)   (State)   (Zip)

WORK DESIRED: FULL-TIME ____   PART-TIME ____   SEASONAL ____   PERMANENT ____   TEMPORARY ____

Do you have any physical handicap which you feel would prevent you from performing certain kinds of work without significantly increasing the hazards to yourself, to others, or to the work facility?   YES ____   NO ____

If YES, describe: ____

Have you had any major illness in the past five (5) years which you feel would prevent you from performing certain kinds of work without significantly increasing the hazards to yourself, to others, or to the work facility?   YES ____   NO ____

If YES, describe: ____

Work time lost in the last two (2) years due to injury (# of days): _______________________________

Have you ever been convicted of a felony?   YES ____   NO ____

If YES, describe: ____

Please indicate the type of work you desire and feel qualified to perform. Indicate your first choice by marking ONLY

ONE (1) of the following: OFFICE/CLERICAL ______   MANUFACTURING ______   SHIPPING/WAREHOUSE ______

CUSTOMER SERVICE ______   OTHER (list): ____

WORK EXPERIENCE List present and past employment, beginning with the most recent (include part-time and seasonal).

COMPANY NAME _______________________________   Describe the work you did. _______________________

ADDRESS _____________________________________   ____

____

PHONE _______________________________________   Employed (month/year)
                                                From _________________________ To _______________

SUPERVISOR __________________________________   Reason for leaving: _____________________________

____

COMPANY NAME _______________________________   Describe the work you did. _______________________

ADDRESS _____________________________________   ____

____

PHONE _______________________________________   Employed (month/year)
                                                From _________________________ To _______________

SUPERVISOR __________________________________   Reason for leaving: _____________________________

____

COMPANY NAME _______________________________   Describe the work you did. _______________________

ADDRESS _____________________________________   ____

____

PHONE _______________________________________   Employed (month/year)
                                                From _________________________ To _______________

SUPERVISOR __________________________________   Reason for leaving: _____________________________

____

REFERENCES List three (do not list relatives).

NAME	ADDRESS	TELEPHONE NUMBER

May we ask your present employer about you?   YES _____   NOT UNTIL I GIVE NOTICE _____

I certify that the information given above
is true to the best of my knowledge.

Signature ___________________________________   Date ____

Parin Products, Inc.

PERSONNEL REQUISITION

JOB TITLE _________________________________ DEPARTMENT _________________________________

SALARY RANGE _________________________________ REQUESTED BY _________________________________

FULL-TIME ______ PART-TIME ______ IF PART-TIME: DAILY HOURS _________________________________

REGULAR ______ TEMPORARY ______ IF TEMPORARY: LENGTH OF EMPLOYMENT _____________________

DATE POSITION IS TO BE FILLED ____
                                          (earliest)   (latest)

Specific job knowledge, experience, skills, licensing, educational background, etc. required (indicate by *) or desirable:

____

____

____

____

____

____

____

Specific duties and responsibilities for this position:

____

____

____

____

____

____

____

____

Department manager _________________________________ Date _________________

Approved by _________________________________ Date _________________

Form 18
Job 2, Unit 7 (p. 61)
91

Form 17
Job 1, Unit 7 (p. 61)
91

NAME _______________________________

REFERENCE NO. _______________________

PHONE _______________________________

AVAILABILITY DATE ___________________

Check one: FULL-TIME ___________

               PART-TIME ___________

NAME _______________________________

REFERENCE NO. _______________________

PHONE _______________________________

AVAILABILITY DATE ___________________

Check one: FULL-TIME ___________

               PART-TIME ___________

NAME _______________________________

REFERENCE NO. _______________________

PHONE _______________________________

AVAILABILITY DATE ___________________

Check one: FULL-TIME ___________

               PART-TIME ___________

(Extra form)

Form 16, Part 4
Test for Unit 6 (p. 58)
93

Form 16, Part 3
Test for Unit 6 (p. 58)
93

Gutierrez Industries
46 Industrial Drive
San Pedro, TX 78616-9216
713-458-0029

PURCHASE ORDER

Purchase order No.

Date

Terms

Ship Via

Quantity	Cat. No.	Description	Price	Total

By _______________________________________ Purchasing Agent

Gutierrez Industries
46 Industrial Drive
San Pedro, TX 78616-9216
713-458-0029

PURCHASE REQUISITION

Deliver to:

Location:

Job No.

Requisition No.

Date

Date Required

Quantity	Description

Requisitioned by: _______________________________________

Martin's Office Supplies
321 Beach Street
Arcadia, WV 25967-3471
304-856-1270

CREDIT MEMORANDUM

Credit memorandum No.

Date

Your order No.

YOUR ACCOUNT HAS BEEN CREDITED FOR:

Quantity	Description	Cat. No.	Unit Price	Amount

Martin's Office Supplies
321 Beach Street
Arcadia, WV 25967-3471
304-856-1270

CREDIT MEMORANDUM

Credit memorandum No.

Date

Your order No.

YOUR ACCOUNT HAS BEEN CREDITED FOR:

Quantity	Description	Cat. No.	Unit Price	Amount

Krantz and Ross, Inc.

696 Tusculum Highway
Arcadia, WV 25967-3558
304-641-9327

69-761
519

_________________19________ No. **2551**

PAY to the order of ___________________________________ $ ________________

____ Dollars

FOR CLASSROOM USE ONLY

Arcadia Regional Bank

ARCADIA, WEST VIRGINIA

⑆0519076⑈⑆ 82⑈5541⑆9

- -

Detach this stub before
cashing this check.

TO

IN PAYMENT OF THE FOLLOWING INVOICES:

Date	Invoice	Amount

Krantz and Ross, Inc.

696 Tusculum Highway
Arcadia, WV 25967-3558
304-641-9327

- -

Krantz and Ross, Inc.

696 Tusculum Highway
Arcadia, WV 25967-3558
304-641-9327

69-761
519

_________________19________ No. **3280**

PAY to the order of ___________________________________ $ ________________

____ Dollars

FOR CLASSROOM USE ONLY

Arcadia Regional Bank

ARCADIA, WEST VIRGINIA

⑆0519076⑈⑆ 82⑈5541⑆9

- -

Detach this stub before
cashing this check.

TO

IN PAYMENT OF THE FOLLOWING INVOICES:

Date	Invoice	Amount

Krantz and Ross, Inc.

696 Tusculum Highway
Arcadia, WV 25967-3558
304-641-9327

Martin's Office Supplies
321 Beach Street
Arcadia, WV 25967-3471
304-856-1270

Invoice

Date

Our Order No.

Cust. Order No.

Terms

Quantity	Description	Unit Price	Total

Krantz and Ross, Inc.
696 Tusculum Highway
Arcadia, WV 25967-3558
304-641-9327

PURCHASE ORDER

Purchase order No.

Date

Terms

Ship Via

Quantity	Cat. No.	Description	Price	Total

By _______________________ Purchasing Agent

Krantz and Ross, Inc.
696 Tusculum Highway
Arcadia, WV 25967-3558
304-641-9327

PURCHASE REQUISITION

Deliver to:

Location:

Job No.

Requisition No.

Date

Date Required

Quantity	Description

Requisitioned by: _______________________

Krantz and Ross, Inc.
696 Tusculum Highway
Arcadia, WV 25967-3558
304-641-9327

PURCHASE REQUISITION

Deliver to:

Location:

Job No.

Requisition No.

Date

Date Required

Quantity	Description

Requisitioned by: _______________________

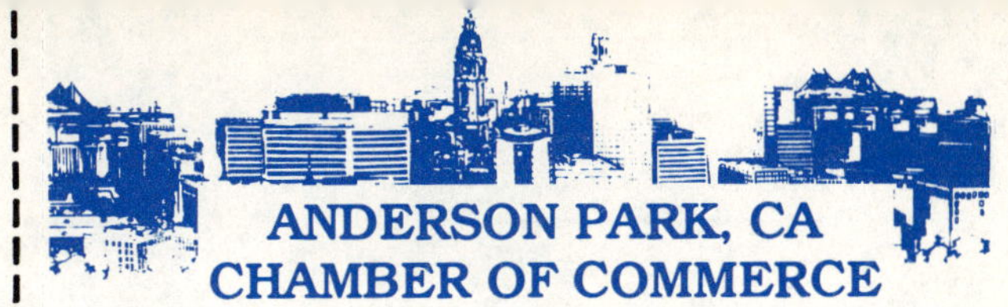

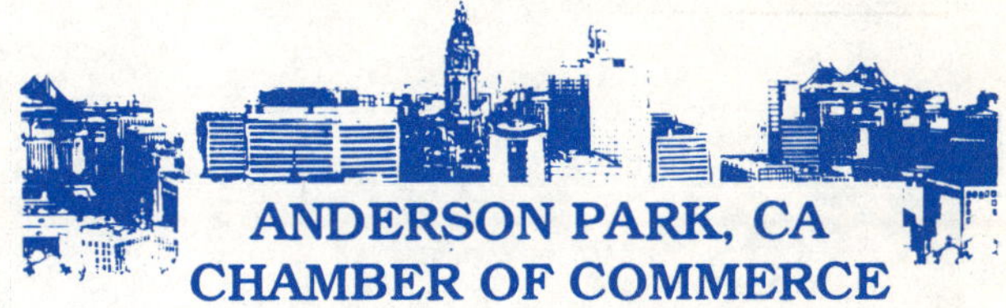

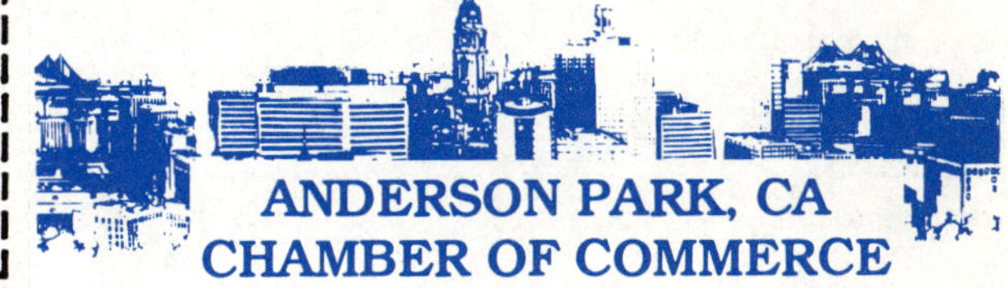

Form 9
Test for Unit 5 (p. 50)
109

Form 8
Job 7, Unit 5 (p. 49)
111

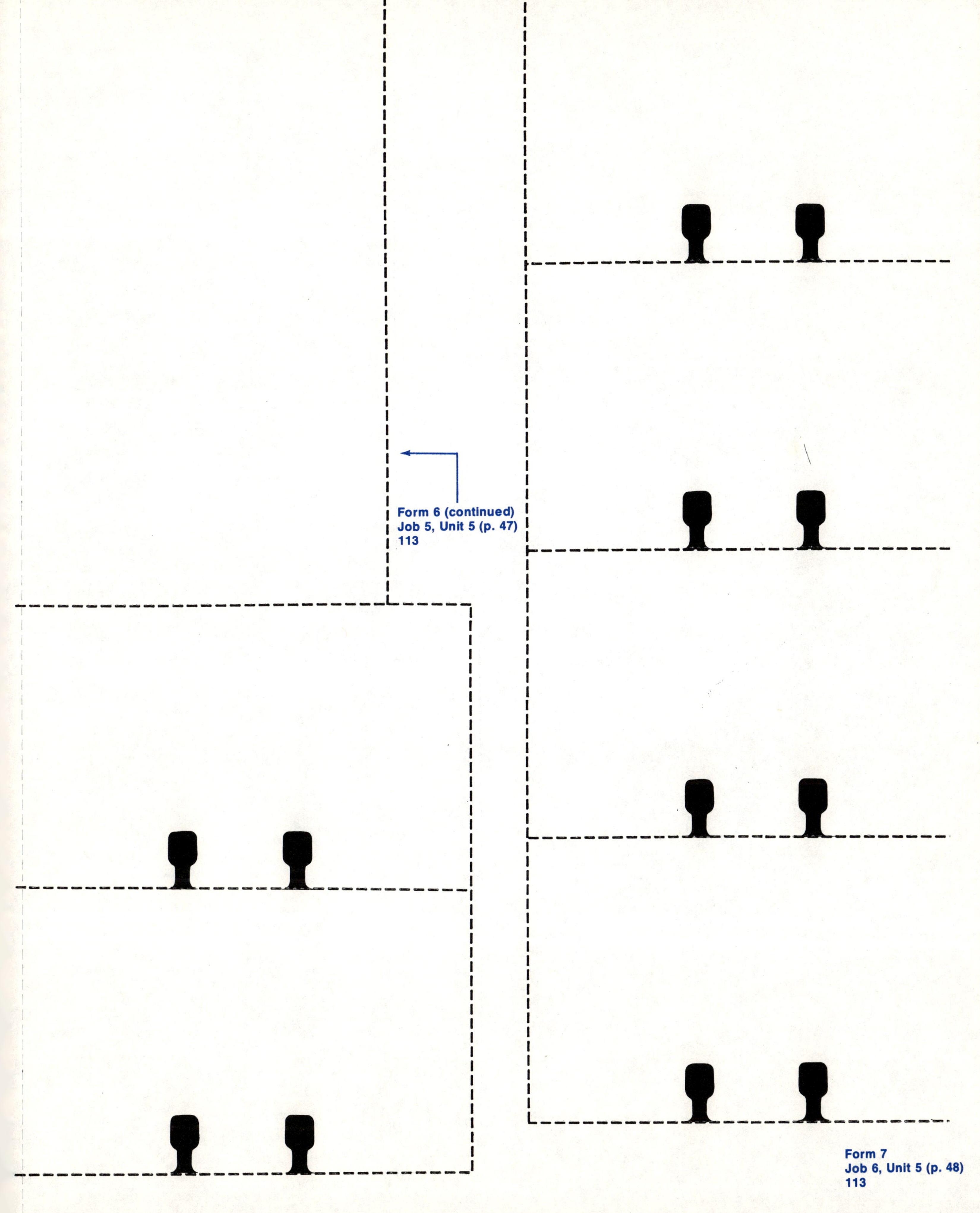

Form 6 (continued)
Job 5, Unit 5 (p. 47)
113
Form 7
Job 6, Unit 5 (p. 48)
113

Video Security Systems, Inc.
Jacksonville, Florida

NATIONAL AUTOMATION CONFERENCE

Name:

Emp. No.:

Dept.:

Badge no. 1

Badge no. 2

Parin Products, Inc.
ANNUAL SALES MEETING
Atlanta

2nd Annual
Cooperative Technicians Convention
Birmingham, Alabama

Badge no. 3

Badge no. 4

Great Graphics

Pete's Stereo

Name:

Dept.:

Emp. No.:

Name:

Emp. No.:

Dept.:

Sounds Great!

Badge no. 5

Badge no. 6

WHOLESALE DIVISION
NDG Semiannual Meeting

Recycled Paper Products Company
Indianapolis Plant No. 2

Name:

Emp. No.:

Dept.:

Badge no. 7

Badge no. 8

Use this form to complete Job 5, Unit 1, according to the instructions on pages 5 and 6. Center each line within the area indicated by the broken line on the form.

____

1. Center and type your name.

------------------------------- (3½")

2. Center and type the name of your school.

--- (4")

3. Center and type today's date.

---------------------------- (3")

4. Center and type the title of your favorite movie.

--- (5")

5. Center and type the title of your favorite book.

--- (5½")